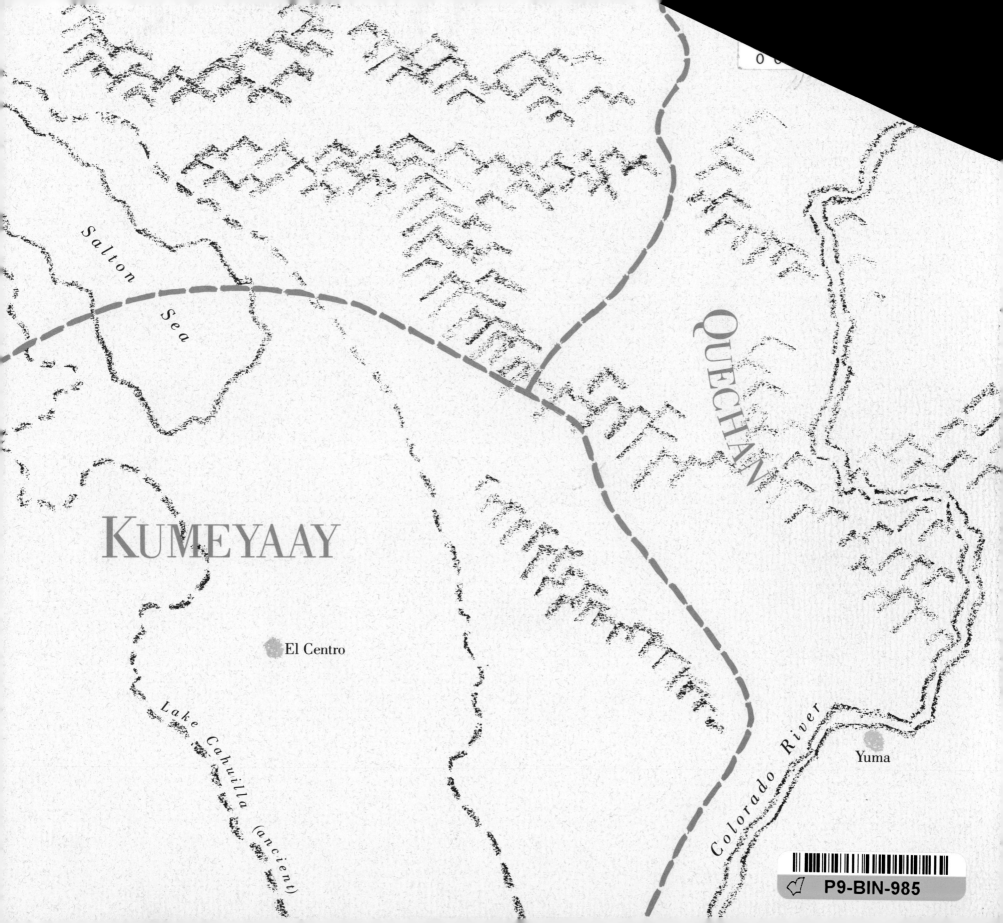

Salton Sea

QUECHAN

KUMEYAAY

El Centro

Lake Cahuilla (ancient)

Colorado River

Yuma

THE
FORGOTTEN
ARTIST

THE FORGOTTEN ARTIST

*Indians of
Anza-Borrego
and
Their Rock Art*

Manfred Knaak

ANZA-BORREGO DESERT NATURAL
HISTORY ASSOCIATION

Borrego Springs, California 92004

Printed in the United States of America

Library of Congress
Cataloging-in-Publication Data

Knaak, Manfred, 1942-
The forgotten artist.

Bibliography: p. 107
Includes index.
1. Indians of North America—
California—Anza-Borrego Desert State
Park—Antiquities.   2. Petroglyphs—
California—Anza-Borrego
Desert State Park.
3. Rock paintings—California—Anza-
Borrego Desert State Park.   4. Indians of
North America—California—Anza-
Borrego Desert State Park—Rites and
ceremonies.   5. Anza-Borrego Desert
State Park (Calif.)—Antiquities.
6. California—Antiquities.   I. Title.
E78.C15K58
1986   979.4'98   86-28863

ISBN 0-910805-03-2
ISBN 0-910805-04-0 (pbk.)

Contents

Foreword

The native inhabitants of California who populated the region before Balboa first sighted the Pacific Ocean in 1513 have left varied indications of their presence. Stone implements, pottery, trails and habitation sites, as well as burials and cremation sites are evidence of the daily life and work of these early people. They left few traces, however, of their mental life: their speculations as to the nature of the universe and their beliefs as to ways by which human beings could establish a relationship to the cosmic forces that controlled their cycle of life and determined the events of birth, sickness, misfortune and death.

Our most likely possibility of looking into the mental processes of these people of the past is to study the preserved designs and figures painted and pecked on the surfaces of rocks. There is an especially impressive series of these in what is now the Anza-Borrego Desert State Park in southern California. Manfred Knaak has spent much time, energy, and thought in discovering, photographing and analyzing perhaps all of those extant in the region.

The interpretation of the motives that occasioned the making of these designs and symbols is an interesting subject for speculation. Much of the lore behind these pictographs and petroglyphs has been either lost or obscured by inventive and often probably erroneous fabrications. The Indians of recent times who have retained some features of their traditional lore can contribute but little to the interpretation of these ancient works of symbolic art.

An interested person of the present has little to assist him in seeking an answer to the problem of what these markings meant to the forgotten artists. His only recourse is to use the logic of analysis and comparison in relation to ethnographic accounts based on the study of living Indians.

The author has summarized and quoted from a variety of sources, anthropological observers and historical philosophers. He adds many of his own interesting proposals. The reader is stimulated to observe, speculate and agree or disagree with many theories and perhaps formulate some of his own. The author has provided a valuable introduction to the ancient symbolic art of one of the most fascinating areas in the West.

SPENCER L. ROGERS

Preface

The Indians of the Anza-Borrego Desert left a legacy of religion, mythology and social customs, some of which is retold in this book. They also left a legacy of art: an open-air gallery of rock art. These petroglyphs and pictographs are eyewitness accounts, vivid on-the-scene reports that give us some idea of what was important to the people who once inhabited this desert.

The rock drawings speak of the soul of man, of his religion and mythology and his inner feelings about the spirits and the universe. Rock art is a testimony of ceremonies, of important historical occasions, as well as of the fears and joys of life. Rock art is also symbolic communication conveying powerful images of the supernatural; it is a mirror, reflecting the complexity of human culture and the intricacies of the mind.

Rock art speaks of the forgotten artist of the Anza-Borrego Desert. Forgotten in the sense that his works of art, displayed on the surfaces of rocks have only in the past twenty-five years been rediscovered and systematically studied.

Archaeologists in past years concentrated their studies of earlier cultures on stone tools and middens. From such evidence, details about diet and hunting patterns could be drawn and important clues to prehistoric societal structures could be extracted. Excavation of burial sites could provide ideas of religious beliefs. However, to learn something of their spiritual life, mythology and thoughts, we must look to some of the rock art they left behind.

Rock art as primitive art is first of all symbolic. The symbols of depicted beings are often taken from the mythology of the Native American. At times, rock art became the record of supernatural experiences of individuals, in which a simple dot, a line, or a circle was used to indicate, symbolically, their supernatural "seeing." It was not public art intended to be seen by everyone.

Petroglyphs and pictographs are often thought of as doodles or scribbles, stylized and abstract motifs too intangible to study or discuss. They cannot be explained. This is the point at which many scholars and laymen go astray. Though rock art has never been easy to understand, neither is the abstract art of the twentieth century. Neither primitive art nor rock art was intended by the artist to be neatly signed and tucked into its correct time period, as is the case with western European art.

One thing the reader will not find in this publication is a detailed description of rock art locations within the Anza-Borrego Desert. It is best to leave them in their sacred obscurity. For those who hike and explore this beautiful desert, a chance find of rock art can heighten the wilderness experience. If you find some remnant of these treasures, we ask you to respect it. It may have little meaning to the viewer, but it is part of the Native American heritage, fading quickly. It is truly art. Much of it was sacred. Treat it with reverence.

Acknowledgments

No one ever writes a book alone. The support from friends and associates who touch the author's life, and the generous help from scholars who offered their knowledge and encouragement, helped make this book possible.

My profound gratitude must first be expressed to the Board of Directors of the Anza-Borrego Desert Natural History Association who, by publishing this book, have allowed me to create reality where only a dream existed.

To five distinguished scholars, all experts in their fields, I wish to extend special thanks. Dr. Spencer L. Rogers, Scientific Director of the San Diego Museum of Man, Emeritus Professor of San Diego State University and formerly my teacher, for three years guided me and read and corrected the manuscript in its early stages. Dr. William J. Wallace, Emeritus Professor, Department of Anthropology, California State University, Long Beach, not only read the manuscript, he helped clarify my understanding of Early Man and Native Americans in southern California with an enlightening discussion. Dr. Philip J. Wilke, Department of Anthropology, University of California Riverside, read the manuscript and shared with me his expert knowledge of Cahuilla prehistory and the Great Basin. Dr. Wilke also kept me fully informed on the progress of the 1984-85 excavation at the Indian Hill Rockshelter. Ken Hedges, Curator of Archaeology and Ethnology, San Diego Museum of Man, shared his extensive knowledge of rock art styles and consulted on the general outline and text of the manuscript. Michael Sampson, California State Archaeologist, supported and encouraged me during the course of this lengthy project.

Grace Johnson, curator of photo archives, and Linda Fisk, Registrar, San Diego Museum of Man, spent much of their time helping me locate early photographs of Native Americans of San Diego County, and Paul Roccoforte's advice and help with my early black and white photographs of rock art made my work much easier.

A special thanks to Michael Donaldson and Sandra Mahan, who did the layout and design of the book. Their sensitivity to the subject and their creative ideas brought long years of labor to a successful completion. I wish to thank Rose Houk for her careful editing of the manuscript and helpful suggestions.

Superintendent Jim Hendrix and Naturalist Mark Jorgensen, of Anza-

Borrego Desert State Park, were unwavering in their support of this project. I am most grateful to them. Mark not only read the manuscript many times, from first rough draft to its completed form, but also spent many hours sharing with me his knowledge of the secrets of this great desert gained during a lifetime of familiarity with Anza-Borrego. It was, for me, one of the most rewarding experiences of the entire endeavor.

Typists Sandra von Herrmann and Donna Gillette coped expertly with my manuscript and made it presentable.

Lastly, without my wife Betsy's untiring patience and loving care during the many years required to bring this book into being, it would not exist.

Prologue

A moonless night surrounded the cavelike rockshelter as a light wind drifted in from the northwest, rustling the dried leaves of nearby brittle bushes. It was the wind spirit of the night rushing in for consultation. Inside

the rockshelter, the old shaman softly sang his sacred tune enticing the spirit to enter his secret place and bring guidance and prophecy. The glow of the embers from the small fire was reflected in the shaman's eyes, unmoving in his red and black painted face. It was a ghostly stare, as if the painted face were just an outer shell, a mask assumed while the shaman's spirit journeyed to another world, a world of the supernatural that only other shamans could see and understand.

The wind spirit turned and twisted at the cave's entrance, stirring up clouds of dust and throwing a shower of sparks into the crisp night air, perhaps testing the depth and dedication of the shaman's self-induced trance.

For hours the shaman sat motionless, murmuring over and over the secret syllables, repeating endlessly the magic phrases. It was still several hours before sunrise when the shaman finished his incantations. The eyes in his painted face softened as his spirit returned from its long journey. From his ceremonial bag the shaman took some tobacco in a tubular stone pipe and lighted it with hot ashes from the fire. Puffs of tobacco smoke drifted upward, bearing with them the shaman's thanks to the wind spirit for his teaching and foretelling.

The old man reached into his ceremonial bag once more, bringing out three small pouches made from deerhide and containing minerals of red and yellow ochre and pieces of charcoal. Each of the colored pigments was mixed with roasted wild cucumber seeds and ground in a special mortar. Now the shaman took the prepared pigments to a specific spot inside the cave and with his fingers painted a large red dot surrounded by circles of black charcoal and yellow ochre.

The crimson light of sunrise was washing up the sky as the shaman painted the last black radiating lines of his colorful design. Seated in a dark corner of the cave, he observed the sun slowly rising over the distant desert mountains. As the first rays fingered the edges of the darkness in the shelter and began to illuminate the freshly painted sunburst, a look of great joy and satisfaction spread over the shaman's face. He had painted exactly what the spirit told him, and he knew that at the next ceremony celebrating the rebirth of the universe, a shaft of light would divide the red ochre image in half, indicating with precise timing the position of the sun. Shortly, warmer and longer days would herald the coming of spring, and a new season of harvesting and ritual would begin.

THE LAND AND ITS PEOPLE

ON THE TRAIL OF EARLY MAN

As the sun on her annual journey approaches the Tropic of Cancer, bringing warmth and longer days to the northern latitudes, the Anza-Borrego Desert becomes a land of searing heat and restless winds. Temperatures can soar as high as 120 degrees Fahrenheit. Silence fills the blistering hot canyons. Trickles of water and small patches of shade spell the difference between survival and death for many living things.

At this time of the year the land awakens to cool vermilion sunrises, and the hot days end in long shadowy sunsets. On occasion, torrential rain falls from towering summer thunderclouds, triggering flows of mud and water that arrange and rearrange the landscape. In these oppressive summer months, the land is without mercy.

This forbidding and seemingly untamed desert wilderness includes a large portion of eastern San Diego County as well as parts of Riverside and Imperial counties in California. It is this geographical entity, this portion of the Colorado Desert, that is locally known as the Anza-Borrego Desert. Its name comes from the 600,000-acre Anza-Borrego Desert State Park.

The land is bordered on the west and north by mountain ranges dotted with oaks and occasional Coulter or pinyon pines. The lower slopes are covered with thick chaparral. These mountains, collectively known as the Peninsular Range, fall sharply to the east in a series of steps, giving way to undulating mud hills or badlands, isolated palm oases, scoured washes, and rolling sand dunes, culminating in a huge depression known as the Salton Trough.

The Salton Trough, much of which is covered today by the waters of the man-made Salton Sea, extends north toward the Coachella Valley as far as Indio, and in the south encompasses the Imperial Valley and stretches into Mexico as the Gulf of California, or the Sea of Cortez. To the east the Salton Trough is bordered by the Little San Bernardino, the Orocopia and the Chocolate mountains.

The present Anza-Borrego Desert is the product of a rather recent evolutionary development which started in Late Pleistocene time, about 10,000 to

The Borrego Badlands are an open picture book of geology.
This ancient landscape unfolds layer upon layer, exposing
several million years of earth history.

15,000 years ago. Two to ten million years ago, active vertical faulting pushed the low mountain ranges that bordered the Salton Trough on the west to even higher elevations. The mountains formed a climatic as well as geological barrier between the land to the east and the Pacific Ocean. Cool, moist ocean breezes were prevented from reaching the trough, creating a rainshadow effect. The geologic uplift, in conjunction with the general drying of the land over millenniums, resulted in the Anza-Borrego Desert as we know it.

Plants and animals have adapted successfully over the years to this harsh, dry environment. Humans also inhabited the land. Mesas are crisscrossed by faintly visible trails. Along these ancient trails rock cairns and sleeping circles dot the desert. Old and slightly modified stone tools, discarded perhaps thousands of years ago, can be found next to these ancient paths.

Early Man left his mark on the land in yet another way, in the form of large-scale art known as intaglios or ground figures. Intaglios found in the Anza-Borrego Desert are several feet long and are heavily eroded by wind and water. Some scholars believe them to be the most ancient art in this desert.

The story of Early Man, however, did not begin here. Thousands of years ago on a cold, drizzly day, as fog drifted in from the Bering Sea, a small group of men and women, with children and a handful of obedient dogs, trekked across a 1,300-mile-wide land bridge in this arctic wilderness.

They were headed south in pursuit of game and unknowingly had entered a continent equal in vastness to the Asian land they had left behind. Mankind had crossed the Rubicon in history. The American continents would never be the same.

These hunters and foragers had brought with them concepts of religion and art and instruments of destruction in the form of stone tools. They used fire, lived in caves and rockshelters, and wore clothes made from the fur and skins of the animals they hunted. Their descendants would inhabit every corner of this new land from Alaska to the tip of South America. The world later would refer to them as American Indians or Native Americans.

Intaglios are a very special type of art in the Anza-Borrego Desert. These enigmatic ground figures were made by scraping the earth clear of small rocks and pebbles, leaving a negative imprint. One of the best times to view these puzzling outlines is when the moon is full, which gives added dimension. Ideally, intaglios should be viewed from the sky. Perhaps, because of their ceremonial significance, these figures may have been intended only for supernatural beings, not for mortals. This may explain their large size and their relative unobtrusiveness.

Although the country that the early migrants had entered was immense and formidable, it was a hunter's paradise. The animals they slaughtered and ate were formidable too: mammoth, mastodon, camels, horses, and bison twice the size of the modern buffalo. The food supply seemed endless 11,000 to 70,000 years ago, and included familiar big game like moose, caribou, musk ox, elk, deer, and mountain sheep. But man had had two million years experience at hunting and being hunted. He was a smart and cunning Nimrod. He was tenacious, but he was also wasteful. The stench of rotten meat from dead bison driven over cliffs sent signals of change across this one-time no-man's land. Hunting sites east of the Rocky Mountains record the bitter harvest of bison, killed for the delicacy of the tongue, the haunch, or some other savored piece of meat.

Thousands of years passed before man started to conserve his natural resources. He recognized the limit of these resources and devised rules, rituals, and taboos so as not to deplete this nurturing land. By the time the first Europeans landed on the shores of America, the Indians had achieved a harmonious relationship with the land. It took only 150 years of European colonization to spoil this delicate balance.

Controversy continues over when man first arrived in the New World, and subsequently in southern California. We know that the land bridge from Asia to Alaska existed about 70,000 years ago, allowing the passage of man and animals into the New World. It was open to passage again 32,000 to 36,000 years ago, and 13,000 to approximately 28,000 years ago. The bridge was severed about 10,000 years ago when the glaciers melted and their captured water returned to the sea. During one of these periods when the land bridge was exposed, people crossed into the New World.

Some scholars have found artifacts they believe date back as far as 40,000 to 70,000 years. We still have no secure evidence that man actually arrived 40,000 years or as early as 70,000 years ago in southern California. Skeletal remains from this area have been redated recently and are much younger than previously reported. The Del Mar skeleton has been dated to 4,900 years ago, the Yuha skeleton from 1,650 to 3,850 years, and the Truckhaven skeleton to only 500 years ago. It appears now that the oldest human remains in California are from the Mostin site, and are about 11,000 years old. Archaeologist Michael J. Moratto writes that a 12,000-year record of New World prehistory is firmly established, but no definite proof older than this is presently known.

Man was tardy in his arrival in the Anza-Borrego Desert. Large game animals apparently had disappeared before he got here. Very old stone tools recovered from the desert are simple, only slightly modified for cutting. They are about twice as large as an adult fist. In 1939 Malcolm Rogers of the Museum of Man in San Diego called these early lithic remains Malpais artifacts. Some scholars believe that these ancient tools represent the earliest archaeological evidence of man inhabiting southern California far in excess of 12,000 years ago. However, the antiquity of these stone tools is not accepted by many archaeologists. Whenever it began, this early culture is thought to have lasted 5,000 to 8,000 years. As the climate began to change, different types of stone tools appeared, perhaps in response to a change in plants and animals. Or they may have been brought in by new migrants with a refined stone tool inventory.

Cairns or heaps of rocks are common here though their purpose and meaning remain mysterious. Some scholars believe that cairns define ancient boundary lines between tribal groups. Others think that cairns may represent sacred shrines. A passerby may have stopped here and placed a rock on top of the pile to thank the spirits for a safe journey.

By about 10,000 years ago, in regions bordering the Anza-Borrego Desert, man had become an expert stone knapper. With a keen eye and a steady hand, he chipped out useful flakes from rocks. Experience had taught him that agate, jasper, chalcedony, and flint fractured cleanly and produced sharp cutting edges. He had a good sense of proportion, too. Stone knives and blades fit snugly into the palm of his hand. He had an eye for the functional aspect of his tools, such as their slicing ability and killing effectiveness.

Years of experimentation on flaked stone produced delicate, balanced points. These increased efficiency and led ultimately to the spear point and dart point. The experimentation culminated in the most effective killing weapon the Native American possessed, the bow and arrow.

What else can we say about these ancient hunters and gatherers? From the scanty material left behind, we know that their life was restless. They were nomads who gathered plants and endlessly pursued large game, waterfowl and fish. Their stay was brief, too. No deep refuse deposits have been located to indicate that they might have lived in one place for any length of time.

Evidence of man's presence 6,000 years ago or earlier is unfortunately hard to find in the Anza-Borrego Desert. Most archaeologists think a site should have a clearly identifiable geologic context; produce definite artifacts or human skeletal material, along with faunal and floral remains; and have substances subject to reliable dating methods.

The Indian Hill Rockshelter is one of the most important archaeological sites in the Anza-Borrego Desert. It provides the first hard evidence of human occupation in this desert dating from about 6,000 years to the present. Work at the rockshelter offers a standard of what archaeologists will accept as reliable methods and techniques in studying Early Man cultures.

The first excavation was undertaken in 1958 by Professor William J. Wallace of the University of Southern California. Two different phases of occupation were discovered starting from a depth of two feet to six feet below the surface. In December 1984, Professor Wallace and his wife Edith spoke with fresh memories about the excavation of 1958, and their excitement as they unearthed the archaeological material. At the deepest level and first phase of human occupation inside Indian Hill Rockshelter, they found projectile points which at the time were classified as Pinto-like points, now reclassified as Elko-eared, 4,000 to 6,000 years old. Their size and weight suggested that they were used as dart points with an atlatl or spearsling, rather than as point tips for arrows. Bighorn sheep and jackrabbit bones were recovered, suggesting the people were active hunters. Many crudely flaked choppers and milling implements were found, indicating that they also gathered plants to eat.

Professor Wallace found a gap in the archaeological material from about A.D. 500 to 1000. This was unfortunate in his view because this was the time the Indians of this area learned to employ the bow and arrow and adjusted their life style to an increasingly arid climate.

The second cultural phase was confined to the upper eighteen inches of the shelter floor. Finds included pottery, small arrowheads classified as Cottonwood triangular and Desert-side-notched, beads, pendants, and a trumpet-shaped clay pipe. This late cultural phase had its beginnings sometime around A.D. 1000, continuing into historic time. Rock art painted in red, black, white, and yellow is located not too far from this shelter. Possibly during this phase the occupants of Indian Hill Rockshelter drew these abstract designs.

In 1774, when the first Spanish explorers entered the Anza-Borrego Desert, the land had been occupied for hundreds of years by Native Americans. Their mythology, folklore and rituals, and the relationship of rock art to these subjects, is the theme of the following pages.

It may seem elementary to mention it, but rock art was made by people. By studying their way of life and their fears and uncertainties about the universe, we may gain glimpses into the mystical realm of rock art.

Mythology and folklore were the unwritten divine laws and commandments for tribes. Mythology tells how the land, the animals, and the people were created. Mythology tells what was sacred, and what was ordinary to the people in their daily lives. Folklore tells how traditional fertility, initiation, and mourning rituals were administered.

Mythology and folklore provide the credentials to the profession of the shaman, and the healing powers he exercised through communication with supernaturals. These credentials gave the shaman the privilege to seek out places imbued with spiritual power no ordinary mortal would dare to visit.

Rock circles are among the most puzzling remains of ancient hunters and gatherers. Made in various sizes and shapes but mostly circular, many of them dot the desert landscape. The circles are either cleared areas or they are surrounded by rocks two to three tiers high. Some are single structures; others occur in small clusters side by side. No one knows for certain why these circles were made, or how old they are. They may have served as anchors for brush shelters.

Claims that man arrived in the Anza-Borrego Desert many thousands of years ago are based upon the discovery of rock circles and crudely shaped stone objects. However, not all archaeologists accept these remains as convincing proof of man's very early entry into this desert.

Tucked into a cave shelter near the Jacumba Mountains is a colorful piece of rock art. The artist used red, black, white, and yellow to express his thoughts in the south-facing alcoves of this shelter. Circular designs in the deep recesses are mixed with other paintings that follow the contours of the cavern. The artist made use of slopes and angles and smooth texture of the rock.

Not far from this colorful pictograph, Professor Philip Wilke of the University of California Riverside, and state archaeologists, have begun to unearth the prehistory of the Anza-Borrego Desert. Two remarkable discoveries were made in 1985 and 1986. First was rock-lined storage cists never before found in this desert. The cists predate pottery which is believed to have arrived in this area from the Colorado River region about A.D. 800 or 1000. Such storage cists are numerous in the Southwest and Great Basin and protected baskets of seeds and flour from rodents.

The second discovery was delicately flaked points in a style known as Elko-eared. Professor Wilke believes them to be 4,000 to 6,000 years old.

This proved undoubtedly that man used the atlatl-dart combination here to hunt large game such as deer and bighorn sheep. Bone fragments dating to 4,050 years were also discovered during this excavation.

Some scholars claim that stone tools collected from the surface of this desert are even more ancient than the excavated material. Known as San Dieguito/Lake Mohave and Pinto tools, their estimated age is between 7,000 and 10,000 years.

Borrego Palm Canyon with four palm groves and more than 700 California fan palms, is a true oasis in Anza-Borrego. This well-watered place was inhabited by the Cahuilla Indians. The pea-sized, dark blue fruit of the fan palm, which ripens in summer, was eaten fresh or dried in the sun and stored in ollas. Cahuilla Chief Patencio recalled that in the old days the shaman burned the fan palms to rid them of insects and to assure a healthy harvest of fruit. Now, the shamans are gone, the insects are back, and the fruit is ruined.

THE CAHUILLA AND CUPEÑO

The deserts, the mountains, and the many watering places of southern California had existed for centuries before the Cahuilla and Cupeño came to call this land their home. This was the land of Mukat, their creator-god.

Mukat's people, the old people of this desert, still remember that long, long ago darkness dwelt in the universe. They talk about this darkness in the wintertime when the nights are long and cold—a time when there was no sun, no earth, no stars, and no moon. Two large eggs appeared out of the murk of this shrouded universe. From these eggs hatched the twin creator-gods of the world, Mukat and Tamaioit.

As darkness still surrounded them, the two men decided to smoke to remove this darkness, just as medicine men smoke to remove disease. Both reached into their hearts and brought forth tobacco and pipes. Mukat took from his heart the sun to light the tobacco. In silence they smoked; puffs drifting upwards formed clouds in the darkness.

Mukat and Tamaioit decided to create the earth. They first took a substance from their hearts to make a giant pole that became the roots of the earth. Then they brought forth snakes, giant boulders, and spiders to spin great webs to hold up this long staff that would become the earth. A great cloud of dark smoke suddenly appeared, representing all the illnesses that would afflict mankind. Mukat told his brother that special powers would be given to a few men and women, who would cure many of these sicknesses. Then they created the four cardinal directions and drew some dirt from their hearts for the earth that would be.

Tamaioit then took from his heart a great wide ocean to surround the earth and hold it in place. They drew the sky from their hearts, but the sky was weak and faltered. After much discussion they created the stars to pin the sky above and to have some light in the darkness.

Both brothers decided to create the animals of the earth. Tamaioit took Coyote from his heart. He became the first assistant and was the first animal to be created. Mukat fashioned the great horned owl, who could see in the dark and help him while he worked. With the rest of the animals created and distributed throughout the earth, Mukat and Tamaioit began to model man.

Tamaioit made people who had faces on both sides, no backs or shoulders, toes pointing in both directions, with fingers and toes all webbed. Working in the dark, Mukat created Moonmaiden, and as light shone on Tamaioit's creation, his brother considered them to be very ugly and displeasing. Both quarreled violently about how best to create man. Tamaioit, angry over his brother's comments, vanished into the ground with his people, and a tremendous earthquake shook the earth. Mountains rose, and the waters of the ocean overflowed, creating the rivers and streams. With Tamaioit gone, Mukat and his people lived together in one big house.

However, Mukat had done three things which had made the people very angry. He had driven away Moonmaiden by offending her. He had given Rattlesnake teeth with poison where there was none before. Now the people had bows and arrows to kill each other. The people felt betrayed and thought that there was nothing else they could do but to kill Mukat. Lizard, often recorded in rock art drawings, kept watch all night and saw Mukat in his big house light his pipe, and blow magic smoke over the people three times, making sure that everyone was soundly sleeping. Mukat then left the big house and walked over to the water to defecate. He listened as his droppings hit the water three times, and returned to his house.

Lizard reported what he had seen the previous night and plans were made to send Frog. Frog, having the power to bewitch, hid out the following night where Mukat had gone before. Not hearing his droppings fall into the water, Mukat suddenly realized that something was making him very sick and weak, and he felt as if his soul had left him. With his cane he probed the ground and in the process scratched Frog three times on his back. These scratch marks can still be seen today.

Mukat returned to his house and asked the people to help him get well again. But he realized that all had left him and that he would soon die. He told his people that they should hold an annual mourning ceremony for the dead. He showed them how to make the effigies of the departed, and how to dance with them so the spirits of the dead would return for the duration of the ceremony. After these instructions he sent Coyote to the east to catch fire to light the funeral pyre. Mukat started to sing sacred songs so that his soul would go east to the Land of the Spirits, and as he sang he died. This is how the earth, the animals, and Mukat's people, the Cahuilla and Cupeño, were created.

Their homeland at one time reached as far north as the San Bernardino Mountains. In the west it extended to the present-day town of Riverside, then south to the community of Idyllwild and past the eastern foothills of Palomar Mountain, to the desert hamlet of Borrego Springs. Their territory continued easterly across the Salton Trough towards the Chocolate Mountains. This was the land of Mukat, from below sea level to the heights of Mount San Jacinto at 10,804 feet.

The Cahuilla and Cupeño belong to the Shoshonean language family, a term used for languages spoken in the Great Basin. Included are the Ute, Paiute, and Shoshone, as well as the Comanche of the southern Plains. The Cahuilla were divided into three groups according to their geographical locations. The group inhabiting the San Gorgonio Pass was known as the Pass Cahuilla, and people

Culp Valley, at 3,400 feet above sea level, is a transition zone of desert plant life and high chaparral. Yucca, buckwheat, desert plum, Mormon tea, and sumac were harvested by the Cahuilla and Cupeño people in this "edge" area.

living in the Coachella Valley were referred to as the Desert Cahuilla. The Santa Rosa and San Jacinto mountains, Coyote Canyon, Rockhouse Basin, and Borrego Valley belonged to the Mountain Cahuilla. The Cupeño lived west of them, at Lost Valley, Hot Springs Mountain, and in the open country near Warner Springs. Trails crossing this large and open land served as communication channels and trade routes. Unusual boulders along these paths often have designs pecked or abraded into their surfaces. Such rock art sites may have been trail shrines.

The Cupeño who lived in the high country gathered acorns, hunted deer, and harvested weeds, seeds, and grasses. Unlike their desert neighbors, whose homes were constructed of palm fronds or tules over mesquite beams,

If there is a plant in this desert which has beauty and majesty, it is the California fan palm. Indians, prospectors, and settlers have sat in the shade of its leafy fronds in which tree frogs and orioles make their home.

the Cupeño had circular, semisubterranean, and earth-covered lodges. Their social, religious, ceremonial, and migration stories, however, are deeply rooted in Cahuilla tradition.

Archaeologists believe that the Cahuilla and Cupeño migrated out of the Great Basin area at least several hundred years ago. Professor Philip Wilke expressed the opinion that oral history places the Cahuilla to at least A.D. 1000 in this area. He suggests an arrival as long ago as A.D. 500 or earlier. Oral tradition tells of numerous village sites in the Coachella Valley and in the mountain region. It tells about the settlements along the shorelines of ancient Lake Cahuilla when it was filled with fish, and about the annual migration of large numbers of ducks and geese. Fishweirs, made of rocks arranged in semicircles and found at the edges of the receding water line, are visible artifacts of these early fishermen. As the ancient lake dried up around A.D. 1500, Mukat's people began to resettle.

Some experimented with rudimentary agriculture near the lake, while others built walk-in water wells up to twenty feet deep for permanent water sources. A third group wandered into the Santa Rosa Mountains, setting up large, permanent villages in Coyote Canyon, Rockhouse and Borrego valleys. Rockhouse Valley and Coyote Canyon were important social centers with villages and year-round water sources. Today, several springs are dry in the Rockhouse Valley, but old house ruins of these one-time inhabitants can still be seen in this valley as rectangular stone enclosures. Historian Lester Reed wrote that the last Cahuilla to live in Rockhouse Valley was Calistro Torte, born near Hidden Spring. His father, Manuel Torte, was the Chief of the Rockhouse Valley Indians, and the remains of the rockhouse is that of the Torte family.

Mukat's people were seasonal hunters and gatherers. Hunting bighorn sheep and mule deer or digging up roots and tubers were all dictated by the changing of the seasons.

Winter, with its long nights and short days, provided time to observe some of the most important ceremonies. The winter solstice day started the New Year. The mourning or annual *nukil* ceremony was held for those who died during the previous year. It was a time to ritually rejuvenate the universe, to ask the spirits for good luck and a rich harvest for the coming year. Winter was a lean time. The amount of food depended on what had been gathered and stored during the previous months: acorns, pinyon nuts, and mesquite beans.

The arrival of spring produced a multitude of plant foods for harvest. Honey mesquite blossoms were picked and roasted in a pit of heated stones, then pressed into balls and stored for later use. Flower buds of various cacti were collected and parboiled to remove the bitterness. The pads of the beaver-tail cactus were gathered throughout spring and into early summer. Blossoms

Deer and bighorn sheep were major game resources for the natives of the Anza-Borrego Desert. Hunting blinds from which to stalk game can still be seen along well-worn game trails.

of the ocotillo could be eaten fresh or made into a savory drink by soaking the flowers in cold water for a day. Young roots of arrowweed were roasted, the bulbs of the desert lily were eaten raw or baked, and the tuberlike underground stems of broomrape were dug up and baked in hot coals. Agave, a main food resource in winter, continued to be a staple in springtime. For the Indians the desert was a large market of vegetables and legumes.

Petroglyph designs such as this one are found throughout the Great Basin, and are indications of an ancient and widespread cultural tradition.

In summer, the greatest diversity of plant foods became available, from the desert floor of Borrego Valley to the highest ridges of the Santa Rosa and San Jacinto mountains. Gathering honey mesquite beans was the most important summer activity, and Borrego Valley once was thick with mesquite groves. The beans were harvested whole and stored in elevated granaries. The bean pods were ground in wooden mortars made of mesquite or cottonwood stumps. Wild plum and wild apricot, juniper and manzanita berries, jojoba nuts, and chia were collected and stored in ollas or ground to flour for later use. The month of August was the usual time to harvest the pinyon cones. The cones were gathered by the women in baskets and placed into a large pile. A fire was set over them or they were baked in a roasting pit. The heat of the fire opened the green cones and released the pine nuts.

Acorns ripened in October and November and were the staple food for most natives of aboriginal California. Cahuilla living in the mountains depended on acorns, while desert groups had use rights to oak groves, or traded mesquite beans and fan palm fruit for acorns. Acorn groves were owned by the village, while individual trees belonged to families. Milling stones and mortars were usually not too far from such groves. On occasion, large milling rocks have designs pecked into their surfaces. Such drawings are often associated with magic and ritual surrounding food-gathering activities. To ensure a good harvest, the shaman performed rain-producing or rain-preventing rituals just before the acorns were gathered. Once collected, acorns were stored in large above-ground circular basket granaries made of "wormwood" or willow branches. These bins were about thirty inches high and had wide, flat bottoms, and were placed on platforms out of reach of field mice and wood rats.

By December, the rains had revitalized the agave and the annual social and harvesting cycle started anew, with the shaman performing the yearly winter solstice ritual.

Victoria Chutnicut of Wilakal, Los Coyotes Indian Reservation, displays one of her beautiful clay pots.

In 1875 President Ulysses S. Grant set aside land for reservations for the Indians of California. The Los Coyotes Indian Reservation which was established in 1889 borders the Anza-Borrego Desert State Park.

Photograph by Harry T. Bishop, ca. 1925.
Courtesy of the San Diego Museum of Man.

Mercedes Nolasquez making baskets at Warner Hot Springs. Basket making was one of the main occupations of older women, and the art was handed down from grandmother to granddaughter. Baskets were made by coiling small rolls of grass stems over which a thin, pliable stem of sumac was used as a weft. Rattlesnake, plant, and abstract designs decorated these exquisitely made baskets.

Photograph by C.C. Pierce, ca. 1910.
Courtesy of the San Diego Museum of Man.

The life of the Kumeyaay was one of hunting and gathering. In the winter they left their permanent villages in the Laguna Mountains and migrated into Mason Valley where they set up temporary camps.

THE NORTHERN DIEGUEÑO AND KUMEYAAY

In 1769 the Catholic and Spanish colors were proudly displayed from the campanile of the San Diego Mission. The Indians of the region, at first curious bystanders, marveled at the squarish and rectangular-shaped buildings of river cobbles and adobe brick that these new migrants had built along the San Diego River. Their inquisitiveness brought them into contact with the settlers and items of benefit to both were traded.

The superficial tranquility and neighborly relations were soon shattered. The Indians were being taken forcefully from their lands to become laborers for the newcomers. A different faith was taught them, and friendship turned to enmity. The tide of history was running against the so-called Mission Indians. A brief but violent flareup of 600 angry Kumeyaay Indians left the San Diego Mission burned to its foundation. Friar Luis Jayme was martyred on the fateful night of November 5, 1775.

Life was no better for the Indians after the Mexican Revolution of 1821 nor in 1848 when California gained statehood. By 1870 the lives of southern California natives had changed drastically. Their ceremonies, sacred dances and songs, and their rock art were fading into obscurity. Many Indians died of disease. Those who survived adapted to the alien culture and worked as ranch hands or laborers. Their descendants now live on reservations in San Diego, Riverside, and Imperial counties, while others have been absorbed into a European-American pattern of life.

The Kumeyaay, who had rebelled against the Spaniards, and the Northern Diegueño had once inhabited large tracts of coastal, mountain, and desert land in Imperial and San Diego counties. Northern Diegueño territory extended from Agua Hedionda on the Pacific Ocean eastward toward Escondido, to present Lake Henshaw and southeast to San Felipe Creek. From Earthquake and Blair valleys, where they had lived, their land continued west to the town of Julian, ending at the Pacific Ocean near Del Mar. The villages of Mesa Grande and Santa Ysabel were part of Northern Diegueño land.

Storm clouds loom over the Anza-Borrego Desert. The wind, the clouds, the rain, and thunder were spirits; all could talk to man and assist him in his struggle to gain a living from the land.

Agave, or mescal, with its distinct asparagus shaped stalk, was a main food source in the winter and spring. The yellow blossoms were gathered, boiled and eaten immediately, or dried for storage. The stalk, leaves, and heart of the agave were prepared by roasting in a pit for two or three days. The baked agave was then transported in carrying nets or baskets to villages.

The Kumeyaay, or Southern Diegueño, lived along San Diego Bay and inhabited the mountains and eastern desert land immediately south of the Northern Diegueño. Mason Valley, Fish Creek, Vallecito, and Bow Willow were within their domain. To the east, their boundary was marked by the sand hills of Imperial Valley and by Laguna Salada in Baja California. Their tribal land reached approximately seventy-five miles south into Baja to the border of Paipai territory and to the Mission of San Vicente, then west toward the Pacific. Communities in San Diego County such as Jamul and Jacumba were in Kumeyaay land.

Springtime meant a multitude of flowering plants for harvest. The buds of the barrel cactus were gathered by women and placed in a gathering basket. They were eaten fresh, but most often parboiled to remove the bitterness. The long, sharp, stout spines of the cactus served as awls in basket making, and were used to tattoo young girls' chins after their initiation ceremony.

At one time the names Northern Diegueño and Kumeyaay were collectively referred to as Diegueño. It was the term the Spaniards used for Indians of Yuman stock who formerly occupied San Diego County and who were associated with the Mission San Diego de Alcalá.

The Northern Diegueño and Kumeyaay had a seasonal calendar similar to that of the Cahuilla. Except for those living along the coast where fish and other marine animals were plentiful, they depended mainly on plants for food.

In the foothills and higher mountains, acorns of the black oak and sometimes the live oak provided the main staple of diet. The acorns were gathered in late fall, shelled and pounded in mortars to make flour that was heavily leached with water to remove the bitter tannin content. The end product was boiled into mush or baked in earth ovens into tortilla-like bread. Another highly valued food source available in the fall was the pinyon nut. The nuts were either roasted in the cone, consumed raw, or ground into a pastelike meal. Agave and honey mesquite were major food resources in the desert in early spring and summer, as were many other flowering plants and cacti.

In the Imperial Valley the Kumeyaay practiced floodplain agriculture, a technique they adapted from their Quechan neighbors living along the Colorado River. In their fields they grew corn, squash, melons, and gourds. Deer, bighorn sheep, and antelope, as well as numerous small animals, were important supplements to the diets of all natives of this area. Rabbits were the main source of meat, and were also in demand for their pelts, which were

Ollas or pots were manufactured by shaping coiled clay with a paddle and anvil. Painting of pottery was done primarily with red ochre. Most designs were geometric, or simple lines or dots. The prepared pigment was applied with a short piece of cordage made from agave or milkweed fibers.

Courtesy of the San Diego Museum of Man.

made into blankets and garments.

Pottery and baskets made by women were highly developed and skilled arts among the natives of the Anza-Borrego Desert. Ollas or pots were manufactured by the coiled clay and paddle-and-anvil technique. They were made in many shapes and sizes and were light in weight and thin-walled. After the vessels were complete, they were first sun-dried. A preliminary roasting of the pots in a brushpile followed and tested the vessels for any cracks, before they were placed in an open kiln. The pit in which the ollas were deposited for firing was about fourteen to eighteen inches deep and two feet in diameter. The pots were stacked upside down upon small stones lining the bottom of the kiln. Slabs of dry oak bark, yucca or mesquite were placed between the pots and on the outside to completely encircle the ollas. The whole pile was set afire and allowed to burn overnight.

Ceramic decorations were used on all kinds of ollas except cooking and large storage vessels. Decorations were infrequent and consisted primarily of geometric incised or painted designs, similar to those used in rock art. The application of red paint on pots was done first by mixing the pigment with water in which a baked agave had been soaked for several hours. Highly impregnated with sugar from the baked agave, the water was used as a fixative for the paint.

Painting as a whole was a rudimentary skill except for the drawings done by a trained shaman-artist who decorated the rocks for important ceremonial purposes. In such cases, the symbols were often elaborate and carefully executed, covering large areas of rock with an intricate pattern of lines. Red and black pigments were the most common, with white and yellow used to a lesser extent. Colors were also employed as body and face paints for ritual, and for decorating wooden objects.

The prehistory of the Northern Diegueño and Kumeyaay of the Anza-Borrego Desert still needs further research. Archaeological data come primarily from surface collections and a few excavated sites. It is generally believed that 2,000 years ago Yuman-speaking people had occupied the Gila and Colorado river drainages. Gradually migrating westward, the Yumans came into what is now Imperial and San Diego counties and to the coast. At the Pacific Ocean they came into contact with people of an earlier cultural tradition known as the La Jollan. When these two groups first met is not known.

Two recent studies in the Anza-Borrego Desert, one at Mine Canyon and another at Carrizo Gorge, suggest that people occupied these areas 1,100 to 1,200 years ago. Whether the Yuman-speakers moved into this area 1,200 or 2,000 years ago, they certainly brought with them a cultural tradition already heavily influenced by neighbors in the Southwest and north-western Mexico.

Most natives of southern California, including the Northern Diegueño and Kumeyaay, have similar interpretations of their mythological origins. Anthropologist Alfred Kroeber wrote that their legend of the beginning of the world involves two brothers born at the bottom of the sea. They were known by various names: the older was Tuchaipa, also known as Chaipa-Komat or Chakumat, and the younger was Kokomat.

As both brothers emerged from the sea, Kokomat was blinded by the salt water. Kokomat accused his older brother of doing wrong in telling him to keep his eyes open as they swam through the salt water, and they started to quarrel. With a piece of yellow clay, Tuchaipa started to make mankind. Knowing this, the younger brother also attempted to model man of clay, but his creations were misshapen individuals who turned into web-footed birds. Frustrated by his failure to create figures as beautiful as those of Tuchaipa's, Kokomat returned into the earth beneath the sea. Earthquakes are attributed to him as he moves about below the surface.

Morteros, or grinding holes, to process plant foods are common archaeological remains of past cultures in this desert.

Malcolm Rogers tells another version of the creation story recorded from an informant in the Campo area. Chaipa-Komat, the older brother, had created everything. After his younger brother Kokomat descended back into the earth, Chaipa-Komat made the land. He asked the ants to pile dirt high enough to reach above the water. The first land created was the mountain Wikami, in the Mohave Desert on the west side of the Colorado River. Chaipa-Komat, finding the universe too dark, took some yellow clay from the earth, squeezed it into a ball, and threw it into the sky. The pale yellow clay ball became the moon. Yet the light from the moon was not bright enough, so he found some red clay, made it into a ball and threw it into the sky. This was the sun, and it provided plenty of light. Next he created the animals and after that he made man of clay.

Chaipa-Komat, having finished his creation on earth, badly offended his daughter Frog, as animals then were people. Outraged, she swallowed his voidings, causing weakness, sickness, and his eventual death. During Chaipa-Komat's cremation, Coyote jumped over all the animals and people and stole Chaipa-Komat's heart from the funeral pyre and ran off to the east.

Of more recent origin in southern California is the Chinigchinish religion with a central god of the same name. This religion possibly came from the islands of San Clemente and Santa Catalina only about 200 years ago. It was then introduced to the Luiseño, who lived to the northwest of Anza-Borrego. The Luiseño taught Chinigchinish and its new style of dancing to the Cupeño at Warner's Ranch and to the Northern Diegueño at Mesa Grande and Santa Ysabel. The Mountain Cahuilla and the Kumeyaay were influenced to a lesser degree by this messianic movement. Membership required obedience, fasting and self-sacrifice. To the disobedient, Chinigchinish would send the avengers Rattlesnake, Spider, and Bear to do bodily harm. Rock art in Luiseño territory often depicts the rattlesnake motif, which may be related to the Chinigchinish religion. Rattlesnake designs have also been observed in Northern Diegueño, Cahuilla, and Cupeño rock art.

The greatest influence the Luiseño had on the Indians of the Anza-Borrego Desert was spreading the toloache ceremony to them. Toloache was the heart of the Chinigchinish religion and was practiced by all groups in this area. Jimsonweed, or datura, was the plant used in this ritual. Its hallucinogenic properties were used by the shaman in rituals and curing ceremonies and in initiation rites for young boys.

Indian rock painting was personal and often sacred art. Its exact meaning was known only to the artist. When he died, the secret of his art went with him. Some natives spent their lives around hidden art but were allowed to see only those drawings that their status or qualifications entitled them to see.

Women such as Louisa Paipa, were a constant source of strength and skills in daily activities. They were the keepers of traditional knowledge for young girls and taught them about food and medicinal herbs, and the duties of mature women.

Owas Hilmawa is shown firing clay pots.

Photograph by Frederick S. Rogers, 1928.
Courtesy of the San Diego Museum of Man.

Lizard was a sacred figure in Indian mythology and a helper to the shaman in the performance of rituals.

DRAWINGS WITH HAMMER AND BRUSH

PETROGLYPHS AND PICTOGRAPHS

Petroglyphs, pictographs…Indian signs that we call rock art. They are the recorded symbols of eventful happenings in the lives of people whose culture, mostly forgotten, is part of the Anza-Borrego Desert.

Designs were carefully pecked into desert-varnished rocks; others in caves and on vertical faces of granite boulders, colorfully painted, strain the capacity of the human imagination to account for their origin, purpose and probable age.

Rock art is ancient art. Its origins are as clouded and as complex as the workings of the human mind. It all started by chance, when humans decided that drawn images were functional and magical.

The first scientific study of American rock art was *Picture Writing of the American Indian* by Garrick Mallery, published in 1893. Mallery was fortunate to record precious and rapidly disappearing information concerning the meaning of pictographs, the use of color symbolism and the importance of religion to the many vanishing tribes of North America. His publication still serves as a monumental guide to the subject of rock art.

For the next thirty-six years anthropologists had little interest in the study of rock art. The attitude expressed by the former chairman of the department of anthropology at Columbia University, Franz Boas, stifled investigations. Boas stated that pictographic representation by the Plains Indians "never rises to the dignity of an art."

In 1929 Julian Steward revived the investigation of rock drawings and recognized them as part of Native American heritage, just as paleolithic cave paintings in Europe are part of western civilization's inheritance. In his publication he examined rock art and its geographic distribution in relation to cultural groups.

Archaeologists Robert Heizer and Martin Baumhoff published their findings of rock art of Nevada and eastern California in 1962, and concluded that rock drawings were made as hunting magic to increase the quantity of game. Campbell Grant, artist and long-time student of rock painting of the

Chumash, proposed in 1965 that rock art was painted for ceremonies and ritual. Ken Hedges published in 1973 a similar account of rock drawings of the Indians in San Diego County. Many articles have since been written on rock art, but interpretations are still in a crucible being severely tested by anthropologists and art historians alike.

Rock art in the Anza-Borrego Desert is primarily symbolic art. Occasionally a rock art drawing depicts something less abstract, such as a rider on horseback, perhaps commemorating an historical event, but most are abstract illustrations that may represent visions or dreams of the artist.

Indian artists of Anza-Borrego used two different methods of drawing on stone. The first involved actually engraving the surface of rocks, resulting in designs known as *petroglyphs*. In the second and more common method, colored minerals were mixed with a binder. Designs were then painted on the surface of rocks. These are *pictographs*.

Carving or engraving rock surfaces is an ancient tradition and examples have been found worldwide. In Europe, petroglyphs date back approximately 35,000 years. In the United States, such art is located primarily in the Southwest and in the Great Basin, and approaches an antiquity of 4,000 years or more. Engravings were commonly made on volcanic basalt, sandstone, and granite rocks.

In making a petroglyph, the artist selected a fist-sized stone that fit snugly into the palm of his hand. He checked the rock for its hardness and shaped the stone into a blunted or pointed implement. He then carefully pecked or abraded his chosen design into the rock surface. For precise control, a hammerstone and a stone chisel were used to enhance the outlines and details of the drawing, producing a stark contrast with the dark patinated surface of the rock.

In the Anza-Borrego Desert petroglyphs are located predominantly in the north and are of rectilinear and curvilinear design with a few humanlike drawings. Pictographs are most often found in the southern region of Anza-Borrego and are painted in four colors. The most commonly applied color was red, ranging from bright vermilion to dull brown. A large percentage of rock painting was done in black, and sometimes yellow and white appear.

In preparing red paint, the artist used hematite or red iron oxide and the oil of roasted wild cucumber kernels. The cucumber seeds were ground together with the mineral in a small mortar, with pitch from spruce or pine trees as the binding agent. To make black paint, wild cucumber seeds were roasted and charred on a piece of burning oak bark, then ground and mixed with manganese oxide or charcoal. Yellow paint was made from yellow ochre or limonite, and white came from deposits of gypsum and white ash. Often the mineral pigments were ground and molded into cakes and stored. If needed, they were reground and mixed. Other binding agents were employed such as animal and vegetable oil, blood, urine, and egg whites.

Wild cucumber seeds crushed or roasted were mixed with earthen minerals and used as a binder in the painting of pictographs.

Once the draftsman had prepared the paint, it was applied to the rock surface by using pointed sticks dipped into the mixed pigments. Sometimes a brush made from long strands of yucca or agave fibers was used. Other times the artist simply used his fingers. It is likely that all three methods were practiced in Anza-Borrego.

For many interested in rock art, the question that may arise is why primitive man drew on rocks. Certainly, stones were a readily available material. More important, rocks were enduring and were considered permanent geographical features.

It was in caves and among large rock piles that the supernaturals dwelt. Certain boulders and outcrops were endowed with religious or magical powers. They were identified as sacred places and often revealed their location to persons with a knowledge of the supernatural, especially to the shaman in his dream time.

To primitive man anything could take on symbolic significance, including the sun, moon, plants, animals, rocks, and even man-made abstract forms on boulders. The artist sought to reveal the spirit of the rock and he was able, through his art, to make that spirit visible.

As difficult as interpreting rock art is, dating it, despite the wide variety of methods employed, is equally difficult.

Radiocarbon dating, the most accurate in establishing a relative age, has been of little help. Items such as fossilized vegetation, bone, and charcoal, necessary for this type of analysis, are seldom recovered at sites with petroglyphs or pictographs.

In Anza-Borrego, cultural remains such as stone tools, necklaces, and pottery have been found at abandoned village sites and have been dated from approximately A.D. 1000 to historic times. Encampments where such material has been recovered are often near rock art sites, and a maximum age of 500 to 1,000 years for these rock art drawings is a reasonable proposal.

Superimposition and patination are other methods used by archaeologists to date rock art. Petroglyphs, either pecked, abraded, or scratched, expose the original lighter color of the desert-varnished stones. A black or brown patina of hydrous iron and manganese oxides generally starts to form on the exposed surface. The theory is that the darker the stain, the older the figure. A later superimposed drawing would be of a lighter patina and would indicate that it is more recent than the other drawings. Studies on accurately estimating the age of desert patina are continuing.

Superimposed pictographs are difficult to analyze and their age is often judged on fading and weathering of colors. Calcification from trickles of water and the exfoliation of rock material are also sources of reference. What makes pictographs especially difficult to date is that the original drawings may be quite old, but the designs may have been repainted by the Indians to retain the magic of the symbols.

Dating subject matter in petroglyphs or pictographs is equally challenging, and their meaning and age are very uncertain.

Two uncommon paintings, men on horseback, draw attention to a rock art site at La Puerta Real de San Carlos. December 26, 1775 was a cold, rainy day at La Puerta. The de Anza expedition of 240 men, women, and children, with cattle, mules, and horses, was settling down for the evening. The worst was over. They had conquered the inhospitable Colorado Desert, trekking from marsh to waterhole. The windy stretch through Coyote Canyon was miserable. It had started to rain at nine o'clock in the morning and relentlessly pelted the wet and half-frozen expedition. They were now on the high route, and tomorrow they would begin to weave through the coastal foothills to the San Gabriel Mission.

Not far from La Puerta the Mountain Cahuilla had also bedded down. They had known for some time that a collection of animals accompanied by a couple of hundred people were trespassing on their land. The Cahuilla were a peaceful people. They wanted no confrontation or quarrel with these new-comers. One thing they noticed were men riding on top of stately horses. They also noticed a man in a long robe carrying a wooden staff shaped like a cross.

These newcomers left La Puerta the following day and are remembered in the annals of history as one of the boldest expeditions ever to cross the Colorado Desert. These emigrants later founded a village which would become the city of San Francisco. Their leader, Juan Bautista de Anza, became a recognized figure in the Spanish Empire.

Not far from where these emigrants slept, history may have been recorded as pictographs in A.D. 1775, commemorating the journey of this expedition through Cahuilla land.

Beneath the long afternoon shadows of the Laguna Mountains a pictograph in black and red confronts the undulating hills. This was a busy site in years past. Numerous grinding surfaces are scattered about but the pounding of the pestles has stopped. There are no echoes rising from the valley below but the memories and the spiritual "seeing" of a bygone people are still displayed here as pictographs on the surface of the boulder.

A glimmer of the symbols' meaning comes from the outlines of a bird, drawn in black. According to Kumeyaay legend, a beautiful bird lived here in the waters of the spring, but it was a spirit that could be seen only in a vision.

A solitary boulder stands like a stoic sentinel over the secrets inscribed on its flat and rough surfaces. The lines and circles meander. A humanlike figure is chiseled into the rock. The surface of this boulder is like a huge canvas, seven feet high and thirteen feet wide. The meaning of the drawing remains as unknown as the shadowy artist, who drew with a hammer made of stone instead of a brush.

Anthropomorphs hidden in caves seem to have mystical meanings and were probably painted by the shaman-artist.

The largest rock art site of the western petroglyph style in Anza-Borrego is made up of thirteen different boulders; each bears a variety of abstract symbols. Meandering abraded lines, cross-shaped elements, and geometric, snakelike designs and concentric circles are part of the repertoire. Abstract symbols such as these are found throughout the Great Basin.

ROCK ART STYLES OF ANZA-BORREGO

Art has often been said to have evolved through time from naturalistic to stylized to abstract. Sudden divergences from culturally sanctioned expressions of art have been attributed to new influences from other culture areas. These changes, whether subtle or rapid, occurred frequently and were linked to agricultural people who lived in villages and towns.

In contrast, art forms of seminomadic hunters and gatherers tended to resist change. Examples of this theory are the beautiful naturalistic, multihued paintings of game animals found in caves in Europe. Eight to ten thousand years ago the artist added the hunter and abstract motifs to the art panels, but the drawings remained essentially naturalistic.

In the New World the ancient petroglyphs in the Southwest and the Great Basin were probably made by roving bands of hunting and gathering people. The growth of sedentary village life, particularly among Southwest cultures, seemed to liberate rock art from the hunters' inertia, giving way to new art forms, especially polychrome masks and anthropomorphic figures.

Art historian Sigfried Giedion finds this evolutionary explanation too simple. He does not think that naturalistic art can always be equated with keen hunters, and abstract art with more passive farmers. At the end of the Ice Age the hunter transformed representational art into abstractions just as the early farmers of Samarra did on their ceramic vessels.

Anthropologist Franz Boas, comparing art motifs worldwide, made some remarkable conclusions with regard to art styles. He said that it is impossible to give a satisfactory explanation of the origin of art styles, just as we cannot determine all the psychological and historical conditions that make up language, mythology, and religion. However, it is of great interest to hear the opinion of the North American Indians who create new designs. They call designs of this type dream designs and say that these new motifs appeared in a dream. This explanation of origins of new designs is fairly uniform over the North American continent.

In Anza-Borrego, no evolutionary trend in rock art designs has been identified, but three styles of rock art drawings have been recognized: Western Petroglyph, San Luis Rey, and La Rumorosa. The styles follow the general territorial boundaries of the cultural groups within this desert.

The *western petroglyph* style is widely distributed in eastern California, the Great Basin, and the Southwest. Sometimes referred to as Great Basin Abstract, it is identified by curves and rectangular patterns, natural and stylized representations of bighorn sheep, other animal motifs, and humanlike figures called anthropomorphs. Rock art scholar Polly Schaafsma describes the western petroglyph style as the oldest and most widespread rock art in the Southwest.

In Anza-Borrego this style is found exclusively in the northern section, former Mountain Cahuilla territory. Its age here has not yet been established, but in the Great Basin the western petroglyph style is approximately 4,000 years old or older. Design elements show strong affinities with those of the Great Basin, the heartland of this type. This relationship seems to support the idea that the Cahuilla migrated into Anza-Borrego from the Great Basin about 1,000 to 1,500 years ago, bringing with them modified versions of this style of rock art. However, it is not certain that the Cahuilla made these petroglyphs, as they represent the oldest rock art in this area. One important element of this style, the bighorn sheep motif, has never been discovered in Anza-Borrego.

The Mountain Cahuilla also made pictographs that reflect Luiseño influences. No art style has been designated to these paintings on rock. Only one large pictograph panel and two painted anthropomorphs have been recorded in the northern part of the Anza-Borrego Desert.

The *San Luis Rey* style acts as a wedge separating the western petroglyph and the La Rumorosa styles. At the same time it retains elements of both. In Anza-Borrego it is found in former Northern Diegueño land, dating from about A.D. 1500 into historic times. This style is characterized by predominantly rectilinear motifs in red, including vertical rows of chevrons, dots, Xs, zigzags, and diamonds. Wavy lines often form top and bottom borders. Other painted motifs are concentric circles, animals, and anthropomorphs. The roots of this patterned and rhythmic style, unique in Anza-Borrego, are found among the Luiseño Indians. The Luiseño lived in the vicinity of the San Luis Rey Mission and surrounding areas, including Palomar Mountain and as far east as Lake Henshaw. It is thought that rock art elements common in Luiseño rock painting were incorporated by the Northern Diegueño, as their neighbors exerted a tremendous influence in such matters as religion, ceremonial festivities, and rock art. Similar patterns of art forms are found at the town of Idyllwild in the San Jacinto Mountains, and in one-time Cupeño territory.

The *La Rumorosa* style is associated with the Kumeyaay, whose rock art also dates from approximately A.D. 1500 into historic times. Ken Hedges named this style after the largest known site in Baja California and described it as mainly polychrome, with drawings of anthropomorphs, sunbursts, circles, and abstract elements. The same motifs characterize the style in Anza-Borrego, where it is the most colorful, prolific, and widespread style.

The La Rumorosa style is found in the mountains and deserts on both sides of the U.S.-Mexican border. Paintings emphasize movement and gestures. This style has greater cultural "space" of artistic expression than does the rhythmically patterned San Luis Rey style.

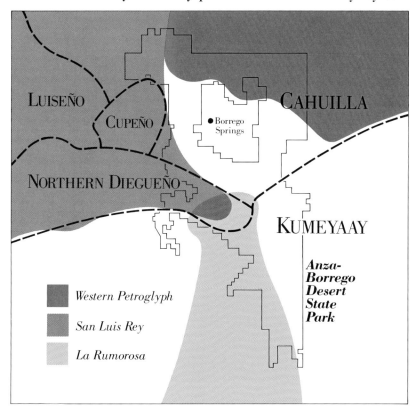

LUISEÑO

CUPEÑO

CAHUILLA

● Borrego
Springs

NORTHERN DIEGUEÑO

KUMEYAAY

**Anza-
Borrego
Desert
State
Park**

Western Petroglyph

San Luis Rey

La Rumorosa

To date there are three distinguishable types or styles of rock art in Anza-Borrego. The classification is tentative and may be revised with the discovery of more rock art sites.

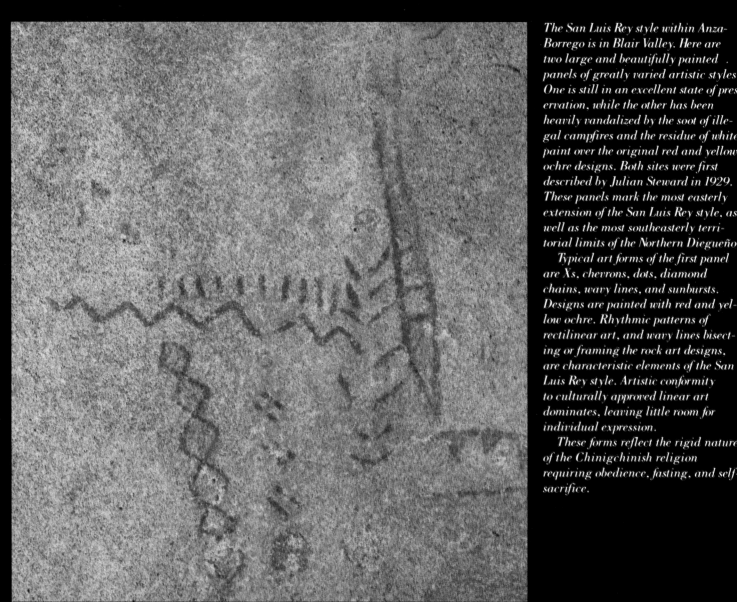

The San Luis Rey style within Anza-
Borrego is in Blair Valley. Here are
two large and beautifully painted .
panels of greatly varied artistic styles.
One is still in an excellent state of pres-
ervation, while the other has been
heavily vandalized by the soot of ille-
gal campfires and the residue of white
paint over the original red and yellow
ochre designs. Both sites were first
described by Julian Steward in 1929.
These panels mark the most easterly
extension of the San Luis Rey style, as
well as the most southeasterly territorial limits of the Northern Diegueño.

Typical art forms of the first panel
are Xs, chevrons, dots, diamond
chains, wavy lines, and sunbursts.
Designs are painted with red and yellow ochre. Rhythmic patterns of
rectilinear art, and wavy lines bisect-
ing or framing the rock art designs,
are characteristic elements of the San
Luis Rey style. Artistic conformity
to culturally approved linear art
dominates, leaving little room for
individual expression.

These forms reflect the rigid nature
of the Chinigchinish religion
requiring obedience, fasting, and self-
sacrifice.

Vivid colors in red, black, yellow and white are a main design element in the La Rumorosa style, and were used to highlight sunbursts, anthropomorphs and geometric motifs.

Sunbursts are a common design in the La Rumorosa style, perhaps indicating the importance of the sun in rituals and daily activities.

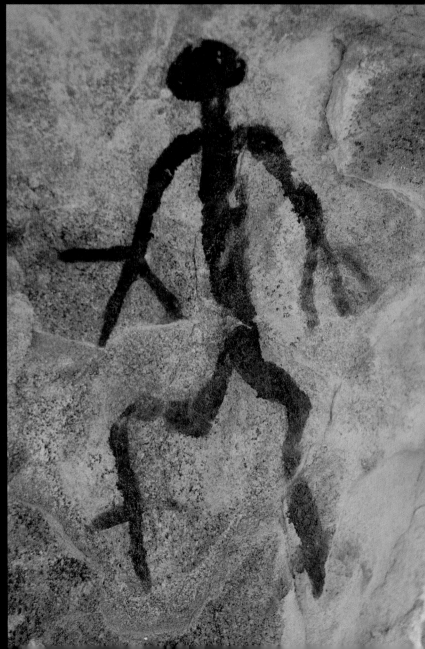

Not only is the quantity of rock art in Anza-Borrego exceptional, but the variety and quality are impressive. One of the most common motifs is humanlike figures in all dimensions and colors. Most are painted red and black. Some are in yellow ochre and a single site has two figures painted in white. The visions of the Kumeyaay shaman-artist are displayed vividly in these images.

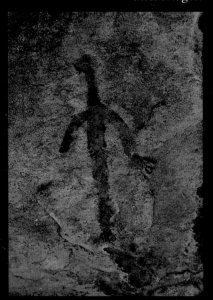

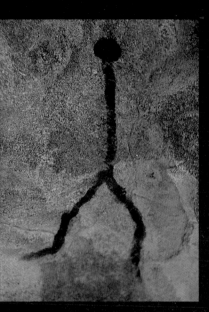

A patina of desert varnish has formed on the abraded outlines, but the sketched image still shows the original light color of the rock surface. Motifs such as this are also located in other parts of the western United States, suggesting an ancient cultural relationship.

SCRIBBLES OR MAGICAL IMAGES?

Rock art has many meanings. For the artists it is sacred or magical, but to some people it is little more than scribbling—Native American graffiti. Whatever its interpretation, rock art is one of mankind's earliest artistic expressions.

Over thousands of years these drawings have been rendered on rock in pecked, scratched, and painted form. How it all began we don't know, just as we don't know the origin of language. What we do know is that rock art was made during performances of ceremonies and was an integral part of the social and religious life of primitive people.

Understanding the beginnings of art has become a major concern to anthropologists and art historians. They have studied contemporary primitive cultures whose social and technological development were similar to that of people living 15,000 to 20,000 years ago. These investigations revealed that their art often is not thought of as something beautiful to look at, but instead as power which can be used to benefit or to harm.

Most of us are familiar with the voodoo practice of piercing an image with a dagger or dart, hoping that this action or sympathetic magic will harm an individual or other being. Sympathetic magic also works on physical items such as locks of hair, nail clippings, and places where people defecate. An example of this belief in sympathetic magic is the death of Mukat, the Cahuilla creator-god, when Frog used his power to make Mukat ill.

In most parts of the world primitive man has tried to work such magic or witchcraft on his adversaries or the animals he hunted. The primitive's mind makes no separation between images and reality. Pictures or figurines were made for desired ends. The individual believed that by creating a copy of the person or animal he could influence its internal "life force."

Many researchers propose that man living in Europe 20,000 years ago made rock paintings or scratchings to represent powerful images for magical functions. In deep caverns, illuminated only by the flicker of torch light, where absolute silence reigns, where the supernatural is most feared and all powerful, drawings made of animals were in themselves a form of magic. Man invented immortal souls for the animals he hunted, which he then captured in painted representations. The hunter believed that he had killed the flesh of the animal but not its soul. The animal was not really dead, but in a changed state of being. Through proper ceremonies during the burial of its bones and viscera, the soul would be reincarnated into the real animal. The final source of life was represented in the bones, where the soul resided and from which it was resurrected.

Such theory has been substantiated by the investigation of the hunting tribes of Siberia, the African Bushmen, and the Aranda of interior South America. In North America, Sir James Frazer wrote, the Minitari Indians believe that the bones of killed bison, divested of flesh, rise again renewed with flesh, and become fat and ready for slaughter the succeeding June. This belief is found among the Dakota, the Eskimo of Baffinland and Hudson Bay, and the Lapps of Europe.

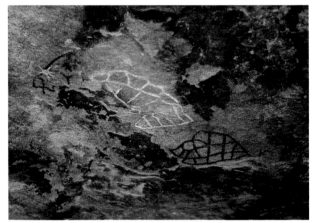

Abstract symbols are a common art theme in Anza-Borrego. Their meanings and beginnings are as mysterious as the paintings themselves. Art historian Sigfried Giedion comments that abstract art came into being with the beginning of art. It has no name. It was simply here.

Early man obviously was interested in his own survival too, and the idea of fertility was highly important to him. Not surprisingly, some of the oldest paintings depict pregnant animals. Primitive man believed that through art and ritual he could favorably influence the generative forces of nature. Such duties would fall on the shaman, mankind's first religious specialist. He provided the communication link between man and the spiritual world. Man brought these beliefs into the New World with him, and used painted or engraved images on rocks to create hunting and fertility magic.

I think that in Anza-Borrego, rock art served many functions in an individual's or the community's life: initiation ceremonies for boys and girls, fertility, marriage, cosmic observations, weather control, visions, good luck signs on trails, and ritual death and mystical resurrection by the shaman. Though we have a good deal of information about these activities gathered by anthropologists at the turn of the century, their relationship with rock art has eluded professionals and laymen alike.

Earlier investigators did not have much luck ferreting out information about aboriginal religion and rock art. They found it shrouded in secrecy, primarily because of the Indians' belief that exposing it would cause it to lose its magic and power.

Friar Boscana, serving at the San Juan Capistrano Mission from 1812 to 1826, wrote that such knowledge was confined to the chiefs and old priests of the tribe. It could be revealed only to their successors who promised not to communicate the secrets to anyone.

Fernando Librado, a Chumash Indian, was interviewed by John Harrington between 1912 and 1915. Harrington said that:

> If a person took toloache and showed his faith, the old people would teach him all those things, but Fernando was familiar with the white people, so they never taught him. The old ones were afraid that the secrets about the poisons and other mysteries would be given away, and they did not want to be punished or maybe even burned at the stake (1981:42).

Historical events also played a large part in the Indians' reticence to speak of their art and religion. In the mid 1700s missionization of California hastened the demise of the local Indian culture. Families, tribes, and old cultural traditions were uprooted and broken. Robbed of land and decimated by disease, Native Americans were reluctant to share sacred knowledge with a people who had brought so much grief.

Thus, interpretation of the rock art of the American Indian is a highly speculative exercise. It is scattered in hundreds of different places on thousands of rocks, its antiquity unknown and the artists forgotten.

Simple bold line drawings of shaman-artists had inspirational qualities, used by artists of the expressionistic movement of the 1930s.

Ritual And Ceremonies Recorded On Stone

FERTILITY SIGNS

Summer. Hot, dry, and dusty. It was on one of those summer days, equipped with map and compass, that I was searching for a reported female fertility sign or yoni. Yoni is a Sanskrit word which in Hindu mythology represents the supreme female organ of generation. It did not take long to find this sacred symbol. As I sat next to it, I could see where the shaman-artist had pecked the rock along the outer margins of the contours to make them conform to a human vulva.

I contemplated this significant symbol for a long time and remembered reading about its possible meaning and sacredness: how it evoked the human concern for survival, the cry for supernatural intervention to cast aside sterility.

Rock art depicting fertility signs of animals and humans has been carved and painted for thousands of years. The oldest known is located in southern France. In the Coso Range in eastern California, petroglyphs depicting pregnant bighorn sheep with unborn young in the mother's womb date to about 4,000 years. Such images painted or carved by the shaman are believed to be filled with powerful supernatural magic which the shaman manipulated to assure fertility and offspring.

Prehistoric artists in Europe represented fertility signs in many different ways: Outlines of nude females were carved into ivory, while antlers or wooden staves were phallic symbols. Bas-reliefs at Laussel, France, and small sculptured Venus figurines from Lespugue, France, and Willendorf, Austria, show greatly enhanced female sex characteristics. Sigfried Giedion wrote of the small Venus figurines as representing potent magic symbols to be used either to bring life to birth or to renew life of the dead. At La Ferrassie, France, a triangular-shaped vulva symbol is carved onto rocks next to cuplike morteros. The production of such sexually enhanced fertility symbols seems to fit primitive man's concept that he could control the "life-force" which existed inside his created models or images.

Female fertility symbols have been located across North America. Although much younger than images discovered in Europe, they are very

Close-up view of yoni. One can readily see the enhanced outlines pecked by human tools. A few feet below the yoni are smooth worn areas that archaeologists call bedrock slicks. On these slicks Native Americans ground and prepared plants for food or drinks and administered the concoction to women to assure fertility and pregnancy.

Here the term yoni is used for natural or enhanced vulva formations as opposed to painted fertility symbols. This yoni measures forty-eight inches long and twenty-one inches wide.

similar. At the Peterborough site in Ottawa, Canada, a petroglyph depicting a figure of a female is modeled around a natural rock fissure that resembles a vulva. Likewise, vulva symbols have been recorded in Anza-Borrego, in Sierra County, California, and Harry Crosby wrote of vulva boulders discovered during his sojourn in Baja California, Mexico. Painted abstract vulva symbols in the Anza-Borrego area are reported here for the first time by the author.

Fertility signs fall basically into three types in Anza-Borrego: (1) yonis eroded and carved into granite by natural forces such as wind and water, (2) pictographs in abstract forms as squares or horseshoe-shaped designs bisected with a single line, and (3) phallic symbols.

American Indian artists were ingenious and resourceful when working with a hard medium such as granite. They incorporated nodules and crevices into the general theme of abstract symbols and used them to highlight sexual symbols of both genders. At Anza-Borrego a unique petroglyph panel shows a phallic anthropomorph, which was first pecked into the rock surface but later painted over with red ochre.

Rock art drawings showing humanlike figures with a phallus are found at many places in the Anza-Borrego Desert. They are usually painted in red or black. Some figures are part of larger panels conceivably showing themes of initiation rites or ritual dancing.

Worldwide studies have shown that man was more concerned with the representation of female fertility in rock art than with phallic symbols. This does not mean that males were not participants in matters of fertility. On the contrary, in primitive societies men were the guardians of magical rites and the keepers of sacrosanct mythological knowledge. It was the male shaman who interpreted magic sex symbols on the surfaces of rocks.

Abstract fertility signs more subtle than yoni require more scrutiny, more conjectural interpretation. In the Jacumba Mountains, I examined two uniquely painted abstract female fertility signs. Both paintings are located on the same boulder, facing east, to greet the crimson rays of sunrise. The colors of the pictographs have dimmed over the decades, but still command the attention of the curious viewer. The most striking of the two is the rectangular motif, painted in hues of red in the center, surrounded by black, with grayish-white framing the design. The second drawing, seven feet away, is painted with red ochre in the center, encircled by gray-white, with a thin red line outlining the pictograph. Both paintings are ten inches long and six inches wide. Ovals and horseshoe-shaped designs are also found in the Jacumba Mountains.

French art historian André Leroi-Gourhan was one of the first scholars to study abstract sex symbols in Europe from paleolithic cave paintings. He divided the symbols into two categories: wide for female, and narrow for male.

The earth was everything to primitive man. She provided him with shelter, food, water, wind, and fire; cardinal directions and seasons for harvesting and ceremonies. She nourished him from early childhood to old age, and gave him a sacred place where he would find eternal rest. She was the mother of generations and in her womb, cut by fissures and crevices, the ancestral spirits dwelt and came forth.

Mother earth was also the basis for religious beliefs, for everything had life and possessed a spiritual force.

It is no accident that primitive man perceived the yoni as a symbol of generation. He believed that spirits dwelt inside these rocks to cure sterility and to help perpetuate his own kind. Spiritual help was usually assured if no special taboos had been broken and the proper ceremonies had been performed. The vulva was part of the whole complex of fertility symbols and procreation rituals. The entire female figure was not important, as the part symbolized the whole.

Wide symbols are oval, rectangular, or key-shaped, similar to those found in Anza-Borrego. Narrow signs are hooks, barbs or dots. Such abstract symbols have been discovered in the Anza-Borrego Desert, but whether they represent phallic symbols is unclear at this time.

Archaeologist Alexander Marshack has some illuminating ideas on female sex symbols. He writes that the vulva became symbolic and so abstract that it could be recognized in a circle with a single dot. Every adult understood the images and the stories were well known in the culture. This accounts for the application of this symbol over many generations, a function so ancient it could be embellished without loss of recognition or meaning.

The most ubiquitous rock art forms in Anza-Borrego are cupules— cuplike depressions pecked into rock surfaces. Randomly pecked into rocks either horizontally or vertically, they dot isolated boulders like pock marks. They are found on rocky outcrops at prehistoric villages and campsites, and occasionally are near pictographs and yonis.

In the New World as well as in Europe cupules are regarded as the earliest rock art. At La Ferrassie, France, a triangular tombstone bears the first man-made cupules from the age of Neanderthal man, approximately 100,000 years ago. Cupules in the Great Basin are 5,000 to 7,000 years old; in Anza-Borrego they are believed to be at least 500 years old, and were still being made in historic times.

Interpretation of cupules varies greatly. Among southern California tribes they have been associated with girls' initiation ceremonies. Among the Indian tribes of northwestern California they were thought to control wind and rain. Another theory comes from desert historian Horace Parker. He said that the Luiseño Indians of Aguanga had a rock with peckings which served as a scorecard for each initiate of the ceremony. Parker was unable to tell if these cupules were for girls or boys.

However, anthropologists Edwin Loeb and Samuel Barrett have left us with one of the best ethnographic descriptions of the meaning and purpose of cupules from the Pomo Indians of California. For the Pomo, certain rocks were held sacred and referred to as baby rocks. These boulders were covered with cuplike depressions and grooves, also known as pit and groove, and were used to cure sterility. Sterility, usually attributed to the female, was curable through the magic properties of these rocks. A childless couple went to the rock to pray for fertility and to partake in a ceremony which included grinding small fragments of the baby rock into a pastelike substance. The paste was used to paint a design on the woman's abdomen and some was inserted into her vagina. Intercourse at this time assured pregnancy due to the magic properties of the rock.

Whatever the interpretation of cupules, we know they represent man's first rock art. The small indented circles are very ancient, and for primitive man they may have produced magic for fertility or control of the weather.

Fertility symbols viewed on a worldwide basis show amazing similarities in spite of great geographical distances and vast age differences. The symbols represent a psychic unity of mankind from Neanderthal Man to contemporary primitive cultures. These symbols faded into obscurity with the dawn of city-states and the arrival of organized religion. The yoni, the painted abstract fertility signs, the phallic symbol, and the cupules, all were understood by primitive man to be symbols of reproductive powers and were believed responsible for his survival.

Vaginal symbols such as this one,
embodied by crevices of rocks, are
thought by some American Indian
groups to be pathways leading to the
spiritual underworld, into the womb
of Mother Earth. Boulders, rocky
hills, and unusual rock formations
were particularly charged with supernatural power and often perceived as
the dwelling place of mythological
ancestors.

To Native Americans a crevice or a
hole in the earth was a pathway used
by the spirits. The belief that spirits
lived in rocks is an ancient shamanistic tradition. Abstract motifs in white,
red, and black are painted on
the lower right of this vulva rock, but
heavy mineral deposits and fading
over many years make them obscure.

In 1933 when Robert Crawford came into Canebrake Canyon to raise cattle, he settled a piece of land already rich in human history. Long before, the Kumeyaay had used the land to harvest the mesquite and agave and to hold fertility rituals. Crawford said that in the 1930s an old shaman told him that if a young married woman was unable to have children, she would be taken with her husband to the magic fertility rocks that are near his eighty-acre homestead. There are scores of yoni rocks in Anza-Borrego. Certain sites were sanctioned by the shamans, but not every yoni rock was sacred, for their special meaning would have been diluted.

*Rock art sites attest to the former
sanctity of the soil and boulders on top
of the Jacumba Mountains. Symbols
are visible from a past when shamans
professed to speak to the spirits.*

*Cupules in the foreground of this
picture hint of bygone fertility rites.
The white-colored and bisected semicircles are probably the fertility signs
of womanhood. The wavy line may
represent a serpent. In aboriginal
societies snakes are frequently associated with fecundity of women.
Kumeyaay folklore says that if a
young woman should dream of a
snake, pregnancy would be assured.*

Constance DuBois, who studied the Indians of San Diego County, wrote in 1908 that the initiation ceremony of young Luiseño girls was accompanied by singing and the ringing of stones. Pitted boulders such as this one may have been used in girls' puberty rites.

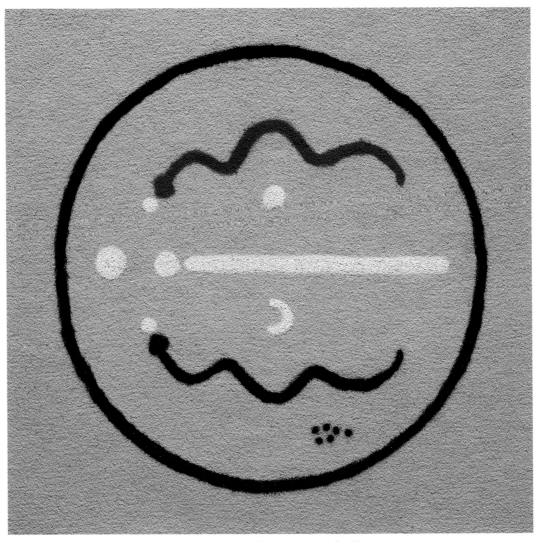

Sand painting was part of initiation ceremonies for boys and girls. There were several styles of sand painting within each tribal group. The painting was prepared by the shaman before it was shown to the neophytes. In silence, the shaman prepared the beautiful designs from a combination of different sand colors and minerals. The painting was a visual prayer.

After the initiates had been instructed about the sacred symbols, the sand painting was destroyed so no one else would see the design.

after Waterman 1910

INITIATION RITES FOR GIRLS AND BOYS

In aboriginal California, adolescent rites were a major public event and involved the drawing of rock art by the young girls and boys. For the young initiates it was a dramatic, traumatic, and unforgettable experience. It was the passing into the serious and responsible life of womanhood or manhood. It was a psychological and physical crisis, similar to a fetus being taken from the warm, protective womb of the mother.

Though the primary goal of the initiation ceremonies was to prepare girls and boys to become full-fledged members of society with adult responsibilities and rights, important differences existed between the two ceremonies.

Girls' rites were a public ceremony, held primarily in the daytime. It was a ceremony to insure a girl's wellbeing as a woman, as a good wife and mother. The ceremony placed the young girl-turned-woman into her traditional role through the teaching of an orderly universe with emphasis on the female role and female symbolism.

In contrast, the boys' ceremony was open to the public only during the first phase of the ritual. It was a nighttime event. After the sacred toloache was drunk, women, children, and non-initiates were excluded. During initiation, boys learned the traditional roles of being a husband and provider for the family, but they were also taught the sacrosanct part of society which few females would ever learn or participate in: the singing of sacred songs, participation in sacred dances, indoctrination into tribal history, the vision quest under the influence of toloache, and the seeing of the guardian spirit and other mythological beings. Thus the initiates learned that the affairs of the sacred world were men's business, the business of women was the mundane "mythological" world.

Girls' initiation rites varied slightly among the different cultural groups of southern California. However, the most important ceremonial features such as the "roasting" of the girl, the study of the ground or sand painting, the painting of the girl's face, and conclusion with painting on rocks or seeing

The American Indian was bound to the land by tradition. The wide open spaces and distant hills where sky and earth met were familiar places with names. The yellow clay and the mineral colors of the earth were mixed together and used as pigments for pictographs, or as body paint for special occasions. The earth and man were of one mind.

The country they lived on was not theirs to sell or to divide; it was the land of their ancestors. The earth and spirits provided nourishment and cause for cyclical ceremonies and atonement. Without the sacred ancestral land, life was empty and of no purpose. This tradition of the sacredness of their homeland was reiterated to young girls and boys at the initiation ceremony.

sacred fertility stones are almost identical in their performance among the groups.

Delfina Cuero, a Kumeyaay woman, reminisced in her autobiography about her girlhood:

> Grandmother told me about what they did to girls as they
> were about to become women. . . . Grandma told me they
> dug a hole, filled it with warm sand and kept the girl in
> there. . . . They would sing about food and see if she would
> get hungry. . . she wasn't allowed to eat. . . . Grandmother
> taught these things about life at the time of a girl's initia-
> tion ceremony. Nobody talked freely about those things. It
> was all in the songs and myths that belonged to the cere-
> mony. . . how to be a good wife, and how to have babies
> and to take care of them was learned. . . at the time when
> a girl became a woman. We were taught about food and
> herbs and how to make things by our mothers and grand-
> mothers all the time. But only at the ceremony for girls
> was the proper time to teach the special things women
> had to know (1968:39-43).

The initiation ceremony took place in the *wamkic*, or ceremonial enclosure, and started with a purifying tobacco drink. The girl's face was painted black and her head was covered with a basket cap and garlands. She was handed a scratching stick and laid face down in the "roasting pit."

This episode of the ceremony, generally referred to as the "roasting of the girl," was the central theme of the initiation rite and lasted four days and three nights. During the nights old men and old women danced around the "roasting pit" and sang songs taught to them by the goddess of the moon when she dwelled among the Cahuilla. In these songs she (Moon) instructed girls how to care for themselves during their menstrual periods.

While she was lying in the pit, two warm stones were placed on her abdomen or between her legs. The stones were considered to help in later years to ease the pain of giving birth or during menstrual periods. The "roasting pit" also played a major role later in a woman's life. She was placed in a warmed pit after having given birth to a child, and warmed stones were placed on her abdomen to ease the pain.

After leaving the "roasting pit" on the fourth day, girls had to abstain from meat, salt, and drinking cold water for several months.

A circular ground or sand painting approximately two to three feet in diameter was shown to the young girls. The outer circle was made in white and represented the Milky Way, the middle was colored red and was referred to as the sky, and the inner circle was painted black and was known as the spirit. The ground painting represented the world. The principal mountains and constellations recognized by the Kumeyaay were painted, as well as mythological creatures such as Coyote, Wolf, Bear, Spider, and Raven.

The sand painting was made to show the relationship of the initiate and the universe. The shaman took the young girl around the painting, explaining all the symbols and warning her to obey all the rules she had learned. He told her about the symbols that would protect her, and others that would harm her if she did not obey the rules.

Constance DuBois in 1908 wrote of a Luiseño female rite:

> A race is then made by the women and the girls, and this ends the ceremony. They run to the appointed hill where the wife of the chief paints the girl's face red, black, and white, and scraping some of the paint from their faces to use it to paint the rock in certain designs. . .the face of the girl is painted each month in a different design and corresponding marks are made upon the rock.

Anthropologist Thomas T. Waterman wrote in 1910 that the presence of pictographs in the territory of the Kumeyaay and Northern Diegueño indicated that some were painted by boys in connection with the toloache ceremony. Whether the Cupeño and Mountain Cahuilla of Anza-Borrego did the same is not known. Lucille Hooper wrote that the last ceremonies among the Cahuilla were probably held in the 1850s or 1860s. This may also be true for the Cupeño.

Initiation rites for boys were held every few years, and had at least four significant events. First, the toloache was drunk, followed by an ordeal with ants. Then the ground or sand painting was made, and the ceremony concluded with a fire dance. Among the Cahuilla the ritual was known as the *Manet* ceremony, which meant "the grass that could talk."

Once the village elders had decided which boys were to be initiated, it was the responsibility of the boys' fathers to teach them the songs of their clan and the "enemy" songs. A ceremonial leader was appointed who took the young boys to a secluded place to practice the dances and songs involved in the ceremony. There, they were indoctrinated into tribal and ceremonial folklore. The dances were performed at night in the ceremonial house, and everyone in the village was invited to participate.

The toloache was prepared by the shaman. The dried datura plant was carefully ground in a special mortar and pestle; water was added to the finely ground powder, and the concoction was poured into a sacred black and red pottery bowl. The shaman passed the bowl to each naked boy, who took sips from it. After each boy had sipped of the toloache, he was seized by participating naked men, and all danced around a central fire until the boys became unconscious. The toloache produced visions similar to those experienced by the shaman and the visions had religious and mythological significance.

Katherine Siva Saubel, a Cahuilla, and Lowell Bean wrote with some interesting insight about this ritual:

> When one considers that datura results in mental images
> of tremendous intensity, it is no wonder that a Cahuilla
> boy after his first vision under its influence became a firm
> believer in the mythic tradition. Datura enabled him
> to glimpse the ultimate reality of creation stories in the
> Cahuilla cosmology. The supernatural beings and aspects
> of the other world that he had been told about since
> childbirth were now brought before his eyes for the ulti-
> mate test, his own empirical examination. He had
> seen them. They were real. (1972:62)

The drinking of the toloache took place on the first evening of the ceremonies and was administered only once. The boys were taken out of the ceremonial house the next day and were hidden in a secluded canyon. In this secret place they learned the mythical part of their culture, including painting on rocks.

This was a time for the master-shaman to observe the young boys, between the ages of nine and fourteen, for their fitness in terms of strength, endurance, interest, intellectual abilities, artistic aptitude, and their tendency to have prophetic dreams. It was a time to bring prospective young boys into the profession of shamanism. Shamanistic vocation was determined by an initiate's communication with the spirits during the toloache drinking, as well as the type of dreams he reported to the master-shaman. Communing with the spirits was a sign that a young man had obtained the proper spiritual condition to transcend the mundane state of humanity and enter the sacred spiritual world.

Part of the indoctrination included ritual shooting of men, cutting off one's tongue, and putting a feather headdress into an open fire without it becoming consumed by the flames. Such performances were central to the initiation process where ritual death and resurrection of the neophyte involved dismemberment and opening the abdomen. It showed the awestruck young boys the magical things a shaman could do.

A separate trial was the ant ordeal. The young boys were laid bare on an anthill inhabited by large red ants or they were placed in shallow pits where each boy was rolled in the ants. This trial would give the boy endurance and bravery. To remove the fiercely biting ants they were given a brush made of nettles.

The sand or ground painting followed next and had the same sacred significance as it had for young girls. It explained the relationship of the initiate to the universe, the mythological creatures, and how the initiate was to adhere to the rules of his cultural group.

The conclusion of the boys' initiation ceremony was the fire dance. A great fire was built outside the ceremonial house and all members of the community were invited to participate. Men and women circled the fire and danced and sang songs. At the height of the occasion, shamans jumped into the fire and kicked the hot coals around with their bare feet without getting burned. With bare hands the men shoved the hot coals to the center of the fire to extinguish it. The shamans jumped on the red embers until the fire was danced out.

This ended the boys' puberty ceremony. They ceremoniously became men and full members of their society.

This rock art site may have been associated with girls' initiation ceremonies. However, the carefully drawn motifs with their fine symmetry speak of a high-quality artist, more so than is usually associated with pictographs created by young girls. In contrast to painting done at the boys' initiation ceremony, rock art by young girls was not secret art. It was public and everyone was allowed to see it.

The diamond chain or "rattlesnake" represented a messenger from the god Chinigchinish, who would punish those who disobeyed his divine laws. Paintings at the conclusion of the rites of passage reaffirmed the final lessons of the ceremonies.

This pictograph panel was first recorded by Malcolm Rogers in the 1930s. Painted in red, the designs have faded over the years. The rock art site is located a short distance from the fertility rocks reported by rancher Robert Crawford. Next to the panel are several cupules, assumed by some researchers to be affiliated with girls' initiation rites. Based on the simplicity of the designs as compared to other rock art panels done by the Kumeyaay artists, this author proposes that the symbols were drawn by young girls during their initiation rite, though no reference to such an account is presently available.

Photos courtesy of the San Diego Museum of Man.

Although fires and repainting by vandals have taken their toll on this red colored rock art panel, the combination of symbols from the western petroglyph and San Luis Rey styles makes it very special. The most unusual element is the hand motif. Campbell Grant noticed that in southern California small hand prints occur with diamond and zig-zag designs and are connected with puberty rites. He thought that hand prints may be a form of signature, and that hand prints found together in great numbers may represent identification with a tribal unit.

In Europe the imprint of a hand appeared first in Aurignacian time, about 30,000 years ago, and color appeared for the first time in art history in paintings of hand motifs.

Hands as magic symbols appear in many different cultures around the world. Hands were used as symbols of strength or shields to ward off danger or evil spirits. The hand gave man the power to make tools and weapons as well as the sensitivity needed for producing delicate rock paintings.

Reproduction of hands on this art panel was done in a positive impression. The hands are covered with red paint and pressed upon the rock surface, in contrast to a negative impression, where the hand is placed on the rock wall and the paint is blown around the outlines of fingers and palm.

Courtesy of the San Diego Museum of Man.

Not far from a former seasonal harvesting site, an impressive rock art site is hidden among a pile of desert-varnished boulders. The bluish-brown patina covering the rocks contrasts with the whitish calcified minerals from rain water. The symbols drawn on the ceiling of this shelter belong to the La Rumorosa style with its emphasis on humanlike figures, sun circles, and other abstract designs. The figures follow the rounded contours and small crevices of the rockshelter.

Color was important to the American Indians, and was used to designate cardinal direction, identify differences in sexes, and to express sacredness in rituals and in painting. This writer believes that a theory proposed by Richard Applegate on Luiseño color symbolism applies. In ritual, black marked the color of non-initiates, and low-status individuals; red was associated with novices in a sacred transition stage. A combination of black, red, and white indicated high ritual status to the individual— perhaps a chief, but especially a shaman.

This pictograph may represent images drawn by young boys or their mentors during the toloache initiation. The color black with which they were allowed to paint seems to indicate that they were still regarded as noninitiates without power. Among the Kumeyaay, the color black was identi-

fied with being male, and each boy after drinking the sacred toloache was painted black from head to foot. Red was a sacred color. It indicated power and sanctity and was reserved for completion of the initiation rites. As the women concluded their puberty ceremony, the initiates' faces were painted red and the same color was used to paint symbols on rocks nearby.

Sunrise over the Fish Creek Mountains as viewed from the solstice observatory.
The view from here opens to the distant horizon, where sky and earth meet.

SKY PEOPLE, GHOST ROADS, AND FLOCKS OF GEESE

Space. Open, unobstructed space, where sky and earth meet, where at night the moon and crystalline stars rise from a flat horizon. By day the sun, considered a god, traverses the firmament carrying a torch of light and illuminates and heats the earth below.

The Chumash, located in the Santa Barbara area, thought that their sun-god was an old manlike being, a widower living in a crystal house with his two daughters. At the end of the day he ate a dinner of human flesh and retired for his nightly game with his partner Golden Eagle. Sky Coyote and Morning Star were the opposing team. Moon kept score. As dawn approached, the game ended and the sun-god again started his voyage across the sky.

For countless centuries American Indians throughout much of southern California monitored the rising and setting sun, the moon, bright stars, planets and constellations. Celestial changes were carefully interpreted and "manipulated" through the celestial power endowed in the shaman-astronomer. As a keen observer of nature, he was well aware of the seasonal changes on earth and the relationship of the heavenly bodies.

One thing he did not imagine was that the movements of celestial bodies were a mere physical act caused by the revolution of the earth. To him, the earth, sun, moon, stars, and clouds were manifestations of spirits who lived within them, conducted business, and performed actions similar to those of man. To maintain a balanced universe and to please the spirits or gods, he deemed it necessary to call on ritual to cope with these phenomena.

Of all bright stars and planets, the sun was venerated as the most important. Indians believed the sun to be an immensely powerful male being who presided over life and death. He was lord of rain and drought, light and darkness, warmth and cold.

The summer and winter solstices, the two extremes of the sun's journey, were precarious times for man and the earth. Should the sun-god stay in the northeast too long it meant days of incessant heat and dryness. The winter solstice caused even greater anxiety. If the sun-god could not be induced to return toward the north, cold days, long nights and eventual total darkness would follow.

The shaman must exercise his supernatural power to prevent cosmic imbalance and death. Since the continuation of life as the Indians knew it was at stake, solstice ceremonies were paramount at this time. The shaman must lay bare and reaffirm his powers before the community.

Friar Boscana wrote of festivities among the Luiseño during solstice ceremonies:

> They observed with great attention and celebrated with
> more pomp the sun's arrival at the Tropic of Capricorn
> than they did his reaching the Tropic of Cancer. . .[T]hey
> were pleased at the sun's approach towards them. Its
> return meant much to them for it ripened their fruits and
> seeds, gave warmth to the atmosphere, and enlivened
> again the fields with beauty and productivity (1933:66).

The winter solstice had more significance to Indians in northern California, while both solstices were observed by tribes in southern California. They had several reasons for keeping track of the sun's travel. In addition to the sun's primary importance, it also acted as a calendar. Winter solstice was the start of the new year. The solstices divided the year into halves for economic, social, and community-related rituals.

Various methods were used to foretell accurately the coming of these events. For the Kumeyaay, the shaman chose an elderly person who was responsible for observing the rising sun in relation to specific geographical features. The Cupeño selected two or three old men who carefully watched the sun and shouted when the longest or shortest day of the year had arrived. The Cahuilla had similar ideas, and observed the rising sun in relation to geographical horizon markers. These indicated when the sun started to swing back onto its northerly journey.

In advance of the solstices certain stars and constellations were observed. The constellation Aguila, with its bright star Altair, signaled the winter solstice. This conspicuous winter constellation is seen on the western horizon just after sunset and before that in the night sky in early fall near the fork of the Milky Way or the Ghost Road. Aguila and a second star in the east, Antares in Scorpio, both gave precise timing of the coming crucial event. On December 21 Altair is just visible in the west after sunset, and Antares just before sunrise in the east.

For the Kumeyaay and Luiseño, Orion's Belt and the Pleiades marked the approach of the summer solstice. The three stars in Orion's Belt were known to the Kumeyaay as the Mountain Sheep. They were depicted in sand painting as three circles or dots in a row. The Pleiades, known as the Hearts of the First People, were shown in sand painting as four stars arranged in a boxlike manner with two additional stars slanted to one side. During June, in the early dawn sky, the first appearance of the Pleiades told of the imminent approach of the solstice, shortly after Orion's Belt disappeared in the morning sky.

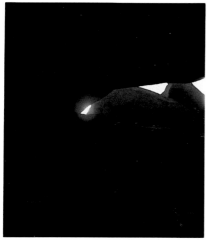

On June 21, 1982, at sunrise, the red-yellow light of the sun brilliantly shone through this small opening, illuminating the inside of this important summer solstice observatory.

In addition to direct observation of the stars and the sun, solstices could be seen indirectly by the way the sun struck an object or rock painting, or the way it cast a shadow on a fixed landmark. Such indirect observations have been made at famous sites in the Southwest including the Casa Grande in Arizona and Hovenweep Castle in Colorado.

In the Viejas and Cowles mountains in Kumeyaay territory, Ken Hedges has observed the rising sun at winter solstice in relation to a cross-shaped rock alignment and a bisected circle.

This author observed the first recorded summer solstice in Kumeyaay land on June 21, 1982. A combination of both direct and indirect methods was used. A small nodule on top of the Fish Creek Mountains serves as a permanent geographical marker. The sun rises directly over this point at the summer solstice. As the sun continues to rise, a beam of sunlight falls through the small crevice of a rockshelter, illuminating the inside and lighting up a prominent anthropomorph painted on the cave's ceiling. The high degree of accuracy in this observation is achieved only if the viewer is sitting directly beneath the anthropomorph and looking through the small crevice toward the Fish Creek Mountains.

Equinox information is not nearly as complete as is that of solstices. Spring and autumn equinoxes likely played an important role in the lives of American Indians, and they deserve more attention. At the autumnal equinox, this writer witnessed a remarkable event. As the sun rose over a distant hill, its crimson rays illuminated a rider on horseback in a pictograph. The rest of the panel remained dark. This illumination occurs only at the equinoxes.

Other stars and constellations were observed by Native Americans, and played significant parts in their mythology. The Luiseño observed Polaris, the North Star, and the Chumash identified it as the one that divides the sun's east and west journey into two parts. It was conceivably one of their sky people — Sky Coyote.

The Big Dipper is described by the Chumash as seven boys who covered their heads with goose feathers. Each night they circled the firepit until they started to fly higher. They continued to fly until they reached the north and were transformed into geese. The Luiseño danced in a circle around the firepit to imitate the movement of the Big Dipper around Polaris. Other tribal groups also believed the Big Dipper to be the constellation of Seven Boys.

The most obvious celestial body observed by all Native Americans of southern California was the moon. The moon, thought to be a female being, was one of the sacred Sky People who lit up the night for the nightly game between the sun-god, Golden Eagle, Sky Coyote, and Morning Star. She was the patron of women and young girls, especially during the menses. She was a timekeeper as well, dividing the year into twelve lunar months which ended with the winter solstice.

Another prominent feature in the night sky was the Milky Way. It not only determined the four cardinal directions but was also filled with supernatural mysteries. It was the symbolic Ghost Road, the place where souls of the deceased would migrate. As the Milky Way's direction across the night sky changed, so did certain rituals and economic and social activities. In summer when the Milky Way points in a northeast to south direction, it was time to give thanks to the earth for a good harvest and for being a good Mother in providing necessary food. As the Milky Way shifted in late fall it was time to collect the last pinyon nuts and acorns. In winter it was regarded as a ghost's road for spirits entering the Land of the Dead. In spring, with the stirring and greening of the earth, a segment of the Milky Way became nearly invisible. By summer the ritual cycles began anew. How the sacred Milky Way was recorded in the rock art of Anza-Borrego is unknown.

This large anthropomorphic figure is the key that unlocked the secrets of the rockshelter; a flash of the sun's brightness illuminated this figure at sunrise at the summer solstice.

8 2

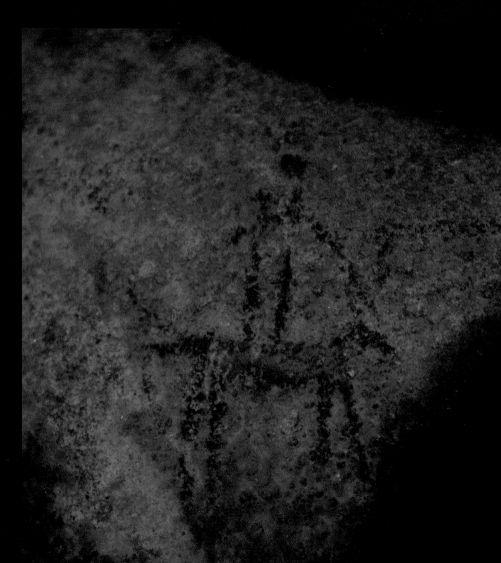

*Observation of the equinoxes and their
relationship to rock art has yet to be
fully explored. Scholars have focused
their attention on ritual of the winter
solstice, one of the most important
annual events among Native
Americans.*

*On September 23, 1984, at sunrise
on the autumnal equinox, I investigated a uniquely painted rock art site.
As the first sunrays fingered across the
horizon, a stylized painted figure of a
man on horseback was illuminated.
One idea is that this horseman may be
a messenger of the Ghost Dance religion that appeared in southern
California in 1891.*

*The Ghost Dance religion was envi-
sioned in 1870, by the Paiute Indian
Wovoka who lived sixty miles south of
Virginia City, Nevada. The doctrine of
this religion underscored the disap-
pearance of white men from the sacred
Indian lands. This revival movement
emphasized old customs and values
and spread like a raging wild fire
southward and northeast across the
Rocky Mountains to the Sioux Nation.
The sparks of this revivalistic fervor
were shamanic messengers travelling
on mule and horseback as well as on
the newly constructed railroads.
James Mooney, expert on the Ghost
Dance religion, reported on this powerful revivalistic movement in 1896.*

A replica of this beautiful rock art panel was made by archaeologist-artist Daniel McCarthy, and can be seen at the Visitor Center in Anza-Borrego Desert State Park.

Courtesy of the San Diego Museum of Man.

White sage, found along the rocky slopes of the Anza-Borrego desert, was an important medicinal and ritual plant for the natives of southern California. The leaves were eaten or smoked, or rubbed on the body in the sweat lodge for physical and spiritual cleansing. Sometimes a tea was brewed from the leaves to treat colds or a stiff neck.

White sage, however, was used primarily as a "powerful" plant in purification rituals. During initiation ceremonies girls and boys were brushed with sage to cleanse them. In cremation and mourning ceremonies, sage served as a purifier and kept harmful spirits away. Delfina Cuero said that in the old days a fire would be built and a large quantity of sage placed on top. The people would lean over the fire to be purified by the smoke. This would help ease the grief over the departure of a dead person.

RITUAL: EVER-PRESENT, ALL IMPORTANT

In the lives of the Indians of California, ritual provided the necessary means and power to control and stabilize an unpredictable universe. The American Indian believed that all things possessed a soul or spirit similar to his own and he felt a kinship with them.

This closeness, which endowed animals with high intelligence and human qualities, is known from studies of mythology which reflect a time when animals occupied the earth before man. These mythological beings lived, felt, and talked like man. They created the earth for man to live on and furnished the necessities and comforts of life such as shelter and fire.

When a Cahuilla man killed a deer, Lowell Bean wrote, he thanked the spirit of the deer for its assistance by singing over the slain body of the animal. This ritual helped the animal's spirit find its way into another world where it reported to other spirit animals about the hunter's activities.

When rituals were performed to thank the spirits, the Indians distinguished between creator-gods, who made and maintained the universe, and the numerous spirits who personified the forces of nature. It was to these second spirits that Native Americans turned on special occasions and for help in the difficulties of daily life. Rituals were performed to thank the spirits at the beginning of harvesting mesquite, agave, pinyon nuts and acorns. These ceremonies, which lasted three days and three nights, also reinforced supernatural beliefs and socially sanctioned restrictions. The ritual was needed to exorcise the threat to health from possibly tainted or diseased food so that the people could eat their harvest without becoming ill.

Almost everywhere in this desert, rain was the factor that determined whether the harvest was good or whether the storage bins would remain empty. Rain was never far from the people's thoughts and with the harvest rites came the rain ceremony. The power to summon rain belonged to the shaman—he was the messenger of the spirits. Rain could equally be discouraged if the necessary rituals and taboos were not observed.

The natives perceived the natural and supernatural worlds as coexisting, inseparably, in a timeless dusk. Their environment was unpredictable, filled with malevolent spirits, simultaneously imaginary and real. Mastering this mysterious, frightening, unknown world and pacifying the spirits was done by assuming disguises and performing rituals. Primitive man believed that his spirit dwelled in his face and that in order to deal adequately with the threatening spirits that surrounded him he must conceal his human countenance. He believed that putting on a mask, painting his body in various colors, and wearing a headdress and a garment to cover his upper torso would give him demonic and supernatural powers.

The earliest shamanistic ritual depicted in rock art is found in a Paleolithic cave at Les Trois Frères in the French Pyrenees, dating to approximately 15,000 years ago. The so-called *Sorcerer* depicts a shaman transforming his human shape into an animal one. Concealments and mimes used in hunting rituals or for appeasing the spirits have been recorded worldwide. In the Southwest, rock art paintings depict Kachinas representing the corn spirits, just as in former times men dressed themselves in costumes representing the Kachina spirits.

While rituals were a daily occurrence, one ceremony was paramount among all the Indians of southern California: the Eagle ceremony or Eagle dance. The eagle was a prominent symbol because it was associated with death and the afterlife. Among the Pueblo people, the eagle symbolized the sun during the winter solstice. To the Cahuilla, the eagle was a great and revered personage since he was one of the original sacred people created by Mukat. The eagle's magical flight was emulated by the shaman who accompanied souls to the Land of the Dead. The shaman dressed as an eagle with an eagle-feathered skirt and cap, and painted uncovered parts of his body in white stripes.

An important and inseparable part of this ritual was the dance and the rhythmic, repetitive, musical sounds. Their function was to awaken the spirit and set the stage for the shaman's transformation as he danced and mimed the flight of the eagle. The monotonous cadence of drums and rattles and human voices stupefied the participants and lifted the shaman into an ecstatic trance-like state. The shaman *became* the eagle.

The culmination of the Eagle ceremony was the symbolic killing of the eagle. It was believed that the eagle allowed himself to be killed each year so that people could be assured of a life after death.

For the Indians of Anza-Borrego, the most important social and religious ritual was the Ceremony of the Dead, often called the Mourning Ceremony or the image-burning ritual. The Mourning Ceremony was usually held one year after a person's death. Not until the ceremony ended was the soul of the departed released from earth's bondage and permitted to enter the Land of the Dead.

Among the Cahuilla this ceremony was their oldest tradition, taught to them by Mukat, and was still being observed in 1958 by Cahuilla living on the Torres-Martinez Reservation and the Morongo Reservation at Banning.

Sweat lodges such as this one offered physical as well as spiritual rejuvenation. Sweating could be prescribed by a shaman as treatment against the pain of rheumatism and arthritis. Rituals involved in preparing for a hunt also were performed in a sweat lodge. As part of the sweat, hunters would rub their bodies with herbs to take on a "natural" smell and to purify themselves.

The Ceremony of the Dead took place in the ceremonial house. It culminated in the disposal of the dead person's property, which had begun immediately after his death. To show sorrow and grief, certain activities were curtailed, women cut their hair, and the home and possessions of the deceased were burned. Several months before the ceremony, the leader of the ritual held council with the village elders to decide on the timing of the event and who should be invited from neighboring villages. The ceremony was a major public affair and required the participation of everyone in the host village to provide food and lodging for the visitors.

Two or three days before the ceremony, relatives made life-sized images of the dead person. New cloth was made for the effigies which were stuffed with grass or reeds. Eyes, nose, and teeth were made from shell. Masks representing women were painted red, the men's black. Women's hair was used to complete the image of the departed.

On the first evening, a great fire was built. As people gathered, the effigies were brought out. The first three nights were devoted to telling creation stories, and the first funeral ceremony was recited. The climax of the ceremony on the last day involved several shamans. After dancing all night until sunrise, they placed the images in a separate brush enclosure which opened toward the east so the soul could make a speedy departure. The dance ended. Relatives said their farewells. Then both the enclosure and the effigies into which the soul of the dead had entered, were burned and the soul began its perilous journey to the Land of the Dead.

One of the greatest displays of artistry achieved by primitive societies was in the making of masked images for rituals and transcendental transformation of the shaman. When the shaman used a shroud and wore the appropriate costume and body paint, he lost his personal identity and received the spirit of the animal or deity he was representing. This transformation was real not only to the wearer of the disguise, but also to the participants of his group.

The Tatahuila dancer of the Kumeyaay wore an eagle feathered skirt and feathered cap during the Eagle ceremony and painted bare parts of his body in white stripes. Other participants in the Eagle ceremony painted themselves in red, black and white dots. The Cahuilla had almost identical costumes, and painted their bodies in a similar way.

Andreas Lommel wrote that the Eskimos see in the shaman's mask a world where there was no difference between man and animals; a world where beings could change their identity at will, into either human or animal form. In rock art, masks representing supernatural deities were expressed as petroglyphs or polychrome pictographs.

In the Pinyon Mountains an unusual masklike human face has been abraded into a large boulder. The lines are simple: two vertical and one horizontal outline the face, and three small circles form the eyes and the mouth. The artist, or idea, may have come from the Southwest, where pictographs and petroglyphs of masks are widespread. Among the Pueblo

Indians of New Mexico and Arizona, masks represented in rock art are thought to be related to the Kachinas, messengers of rain and clouds who lived on mountaintops or at springs.

The abstract symbols in this unusual pictograph at the base of the Laguna Mountains may represent life, death, and resurrection. Only a short distance away are a sacred burial ground and the source for all life in the desert: water.

The colors of this rock art panel range from bright red to dull brown-red to dull yellow. A birdlike motif in red appears next to other ochre painted abstract designs. Birds have always represented shamanic flights from darkness into spiritual lightness.

A red lizardlike design draws attention to two yellow circles. Lizard was a shaman's helper during curing rituals, while circles may symbolize the self: the oneness of mankind with the universe.

The three humanlike skeletal figures are the prominent part of the panel. These so-called X-ray motifs were most often of animals such as fish and deer. The drawings show both internal and external features of the animal, and may represent a form of sympathetic magic associated with hunting rites.

On this panel the X-ray figures are testimony of powerful images representing life, death, and mythical

Cinon Mataweer Duro was the last great shaman of the Northern Diegueño at Mesa Grande. He wears a sacred owl-and-hawk-feather headdress of the toloache shaman, and carries over his shoulder an eagle feather skirt, an important ritual garment.

Photograph by Ed Davis, about 1906/1907.
Courtesy of the San Diego Museum of Man.

SHAMAN, THE MAN WHO SEES BEYOND THE STARS

Raven darkness settles over the village as the shaman is summoned to the sickbed. Inside the circular brush shelter, a partially disrobed patient is lying on rabbit skin blankets. The flicker of fire from the cooking hearth lights the dim recesses of the room, illuminating the pale features of the patient. The air is tense as relatives seated against the wall of the shelter stare in silence at the shaman's preparations. An aura of magic pervades the entire hut.

The patient complains of headaches and severe abdominal pain. The barefooted shaman approaches the sick person and begins to sing softly to summon the helping spirits. He needs to discover if the illness has been caused by the intrusion of some harmful object or by "soul loss." Kneeling beside the patient, he begins his preliminary examination. Gently palpating the area of pain, he blows several breaths over the afflicted area, continuing his message-song. After some time the shaman rises and walks around the hearth clockwise, then counterclockwise. He does this three times.

The relatives of the sick person, who have been singing softly with the shaman to waken the spirits, fall silent. They listen attentively to his special song and watch his theatrical, erratic movements. The shaman, chanting with his eyes half closed, sways back and forth and continues to murmur his sacred tune. The audience knows that he has not yet made contact with the spirits. He starts to sing more forcefully to invite the spirits to come into the home of the patient. The shaman senses the spirits are near, perhaps in the mountains or in the silent night air of the desert.

The shaman repeats his songs ten, twenty, thirty times in short phrases without pause. He sings in a monotonous, hypnotic manner. He begins to feel the presence of the spirits as they approach the inside of the shelter and enter his own body. By his tenseness the audience knows the shaman has made contact with the supernatural. Suddenly the shaman's voice rises to a high pitch. His body shakes and trembles as the powerful and invisible spiritual force takes hold of him. He continues to sing in a quick and jerky voice as he speaks to the spirits and the spirits reply.

Datura, jimsonweed, thornapple, and belladonna are the various names given to this plant of the nightshade family. To the historic natives it was known as yerba del diablo, *the devil's weed. Its beautiful white and purple-tinged, bell-shaped flower and large green leaves belie its true character as a lethal hallucinogenic plant. Datura was powerful medicine. It contains several alkaloids that affect the central nervous system. Scopolamine acts as a depressant and causes drowsiness, sleep, and at times amnesia. Atropine dilates the pupils and affects the muscles of the central nervous system. The combination of these alkaloids made datura an ideal narcotic for ritual use. It induced drowsiness, sleep, and vivid dreams of realistic images believed to be of divine origin. Datura was the oracular medium and guide to the spirit world. It provided the means for a shaman to transcend reality and enter the world of the sacred and supernatural.*

He repeats every word the spirits tell him, intelligible only to him. The spirits reveal to him the cause of the patient's ailment and what the cure will be. The strain on his body is visible. Streams of sweat run down his face and his naked torso as the dialogue continues. Abruptly the shaman stops singing and opens his eyes. He appears to be coming out of a deep trance. He sings softly until he recovers, thanking the spirits for their aid and for their help in curing the patient. He hastens to tell the audience about his ecstatic journey and his encounter with the supernatural helpers. He tells them how he discovered the cause of the illness on his transcendental journey and how the spirits revealed the cure to him.

Now the shaman begins his healing. Relatives of the sick man, watching in the darkness of the shelter, see the unbelievable happen. From behind the neck of the patient the shaman brings forth a small amount of hair. Just above the navel of the sufferer the shaman starts to suck the skin. First he draws blood, then some thick yellow pus that he spits into a small hole in the ground. He repeats the process. Unexpectedly, a small pebble is extracted from the afflicted area. Here is the cause of the illness. He holds it up and shows it to the audience and to the patient. He throws the pebble into the hole and covers it with dirt.

The shaman now asks for his sacred pipe to be filled with tobacco and he begins to smoke, thanking the spirits for their help. Both the pipe and the smoke of the tobacco serve as sacred mediation with and propitiation of the spirits.

The shaman is pleased and proud. His patient is healed and doing well. The anxiety of the relatives has diminished and the cause of the illness has been analyzed to the satisfaction of the community. He has reconfirmed his eminence as a great healer within the tribal group.

The songs and ritual pipe smoking continue for several hours. The shaman gives instructions to the family of the patient on diet and taboos to be observed. He decides the type of curing design that should be painted on the patient's body, a design which he had painted some time ago in a rock shelter, a symbol whose curative powers had proven to be successful. The ceremony ends shortly before dawn.

———

Who was this extraordinary individual who could make an audience believe that pebbles, hair, arrowheads, and even small birds can be extracted from a person's body? What kind of power did he possess to summon the spirits?

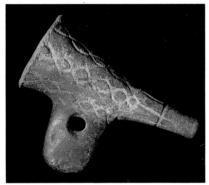

Tobacco had magic. As the light blue smoke from the shaman's lips drifted into the air, people sitting around him knew he was making contact with his spiritual helpers. The pipe and the tobacco were the symbols of a shaman's relationship with the supernatural. Before each ceremony, the shaman blew smoke to the four sacred cardinal directions and to the earth and sky to keep away mischievous spirits that might affect the ritual. Tobacco was smoked in the ceremonial house to drive away evil spirits, and to purify objects that had been tarnished by improper ritual. In curing ceremonies, tobacco was smoked for common sickness or that induced by witchcraft. A shaman's breath mixed with tobacco smoke was a powerful aid in healing. Blowing smoke over the patient purified him and gave the shaman additional power to draw out disease.

What kind of man was a shaman who could stop clouds, bring rain, make prophecies, interpret dreams, descend into the underworld to speak to the souls of the dead, and retrieve the straying souls of the living? How does rock art relate to the art of shamanism? Some of these questions may be answered by tracing the history of shamanism.

Shamanism is a worldwide religious phenomenon as ancient as society itself. Its spiritual roots can be traced to the oldest form of social organization, the hunting culture, in which man's nature was conceived as similar to that of an animal. The interchangeability of the two through disguises such as masks is a characteristic phenomenon of the spiritualism of these cultures and one to which the origin of shamanistic beliefs is attributed.

The word *shaman* comes from the Tungus tribe in Russia where religious life was centered around the shaman, and was first recorded by early visitors to Central Asia. With the exploration of the world by Europeans, similar magico-religious phenomena were observed in North and South America, Oceania, Australia, and Indochina. However, shamanism found its most perfect expression among the hunting tribes of Siberia, the Eskimos, North American Indians, and the Lapps of Northern Europe.

A shaman was a man of many professions. To one patient he might be what we in the western world would refer to as a country doctor, prescribing a hearty dose of herbal medication and lecturing on what to eat. He was a psychiatrist to another patient, diagnosing his mental health and interpreting his dreams. To his cultural group he was the leader of important annual rituals and mourning ceremonies. He served as the medium to the supernatural because he knew the mythical and spiritual world. He was also a dreamer, an artistically creative and productive man. He was an artist.

A shaman's tribe believed him to be a great magician, one who controlled events and could change his being into another form, usually that of a bird or other animal. If a shaman growled or barked like a coyote during his seance, it was said that the spirit of that animal had taken over. He *was* a coyote in the eyes and minds of the onlookers.

The shaman was the center, the brain, and the soul of a community. His function was to predict events, explain natural phenomena, prevent disease of the soul, and balance the cosmos through rituals and ceremonies known only to him.

Curing the sick was the shaman's primary responsibility. For a Cahuilla shaman the obligation was imposed by Mukat, the creator-god. Before Mukat died, he gave special curing powers to certain individuals. Mukat taught the language of animals to these specialists and gave them powers with regard to the spirits and death.

Healing seances, or for that matter most ceremonies, were held at night. It was in the quiet of night that the supernatural forces were most powerful and most readily available to be called on for assistance. To prepare for healing seances the shaman sought solitude; he fasted, and dreamed. It was in dreams that the spirits would reveal themselves and speak to him, and all knowledge was revealed. It may have been during such times that the shaman also painted rock art, symbols which occurred in dreams and served as mnemonic signs for curing rituals. The shaman was not consulted every time an individual had a stomachache or a broken bone. This was left to other specialists with more specific knowledge in treating such symptoms and misfortunes.

A great shaman's healing world was the realm of the psychic. He was a knower of the spirits, and he alone could explain the unexplainable infirmities. Only the shaman could travel and traverse time from the present to the past and into the future. It was a shaman who would be called upon to retrieve a person's lost soul. A soul might be captured by a ghost, evil spirit, or witchcraft. In such cases, a shaman was immediately summoned to search for the lost soul. Such a journey was no easy task as the shaman had to visit the land of the spirits or enter the world of the dead to find the soul and bring it back.

During such transcendental journeys a shaman's soul would separate from his body and fly from the earth to the sky or from the earth to the underworld looking for the lost soul. No one would dare speak or awaken him from his deathlike sleep. Mortals could see nothing of these events; they would see only the shaman's body lying still. But other shamans could see the extraordinary reality. After returning from his flight with the recaptured soul, the shaman would tell tales of his battles with bloodthirsty, man-eating spirits of the underworld, how he had crossed raging streams and deep oceans with danger lurking everywhere. He would mime and gesture his supernatural experiences to his awestruck audience. To the onlookers his stories were reality.

The psychic world of the American Indian of southern California, Spencer Rogers wrote, was a world of supernatural powers and mystic cosmic forces. This world was divided into three layers. The Upper World was inhabited by the primeval spirits and the creator gods. In this case, Mukat and Tamaioit for the Cupeño and Cahuilla, and Tuchaipa and Yokomatis for the Northern Diegueño and Kumeyaay. The sun, moon, and other important spirit entities also lived in the Upper World. The middle layer was the center of the universe. In it were the earth, humans, and the lesser spirits. The lowest tier was that of the underworld. It was pockmarked with caverns and laced with springs. Grotesque and malevolent creatures made their homes here.

Only the shaman knew the mystery of passage along the axis connecting the three tiers of the universe. This corridor was used by the gods to descend to earth and by the dead to descend to the underworld. It was along this path the shaman's soul would go to visit the spirits and the souls of the dead.

Shamanism was a profession that required above-average intelligence to comprehend the mythical world and to understand the concepts of disease. Training was required in the arts, mythology, sleight of hand, history of the tribe, dream analysis, and the use of herbal medicines.

A shaman was chosen by the spirits. This occurred in dreams and the spirits would speak to the dreamer. He could not escape the spirits' call for fear of incurring their wrath. It is said that a true shaman of the Cahuilla was made in the womb by the creator-god. This was also true of the Cupeño shaman, whose early childhood dreams continued throughout his life. These dreams were sent by Mukat, who through his helping spirits, Coyote, Owl and Eagle, would give instruction to the shaman.

Kumeyaay and Northern Diegueño shamans also sometimes received their callings in the womb. If this occurred, these shamans were able to change physical shape. The most powerful were the Bear and Rattlesnake shamans who could change their shapes at will.

More than any other person the shaman was involved with the production and interpretation of rock art. There were several reasons for this. First, rock art was sacred art, imbued with supernatural power that only the shaman could understand. The locations of drawings were sacrosanct and the ordinary tribesmen avoided, feared and were seldom allowed to visit them. Rock art usually included visual representations of the shaman's datura-induced hallucinations. Mythological beings, visions of the supernatural, helping spirits, or other spirit entities may have been symbolically painted or carved on the surfaces of rocks. Only the shaman could paint these mythical beings or primordial spirits. He alone could see them in his dreams. He alone could dare to paint them without incurring their wrath.

Shamanistic art was not concerned with realistic representation but with the spiritual power concealed within the object drawn. Rock art was an art of symbols and its subject matter was drawn from images of myth and magic that were real only to the shaman.

To western viewers, shamanistic art may seem crude, primitive, misshapen and unfinished. Formal expression in drawing as seen in European art was not needed by the native artist. The meaning of his art was contained in its function and did not depend on aesthetics. Shamanistic art represented a higher reality, a transcendental world accessible only through mystical experiences and special techniques.

Shamanism was a learned profession and so was being a master artist. Rock art was not easy to prepare for or draw. The location of a secret place for rock art was revealed only in dreams and visions, and may have taken years to find. If rock art was to signify a solstice site, it had to be oriented in such a way that the sun's rays would illuminate the drawing at sunrise. Some illustrations done by the shaman may have been symbols from the mythical world. Frequent use of datura enabled the shaman to "see" extraordinary reality and create new designs that only he knew.

Painting required patience to find the colored minerals, and knowledge of the right binding medium and how to apply the paint. The proper ingredients were important so that the painting would last for years and not wash away in rain or fade in the intense summer sun.

Applying the color to the hard, granular lithic surface required judgement and forethought about the completed appearance of the rock art panel and how best to achieve it. Figures and symbols were painted along the natural contours of cave recesses to give them an added dimension.

Literature on the shaman, his unique status and unquestioned relationship with the supernatural world, fills hundreds of books. Unfortunately, the relationship of shamanism and rock art has been seriously investigated only during the past twenty years. Certainly one of the most remarkable findings about shamanism is that despite tremendous geographical distances and great cultural diversity, the profession was worldwide. Abstract or stylized drawings on rocks at times have a striking similarity whether they occur in Europe, in Africa, or in Anza-Borrego. Rock art and shamanism comprise one of the oldest cultural continuities between the old and new worlds. The origins of both are obscure and we may never be able to discover them.

Art, mankind's first aesthetic expression, either carved on wood or ivory or engraved or painted on rocks, was part of the cultural inventory of the earliest New World immigrants. The psychic unity of spirituality and art was expressed thousands of years ago by the man with the knowledge and the magic—the shaman. The forgotten artist.

Halos, horns, or wavy lines protruding from the head or body of humanlike figures may be symbols of super- natural powers.

This froglike image, drawn in black, is hidden in a small cave near a stream and a grove of sycamore and cottonwood trees. Frog, a mythological being, was one of the original animal-people in Indian mythology. He was a trickster and had the power to bewitch.

Inside this cave shelter are small morteros on a pancake-shaped boulder. Perhaps the shaman prepared black paint in these small cups, or they may have held the finely ground powder from which the sacred toloache drink was made.

The finest example of humanlike figures is found in the In-Ko-Pah Mountains.
Painted in yellow, the figures are unusually large. Are they mythological beings
or are they spirit helpers? Who was the forgotten artist? The answer is forever
sealed within these granitic walls where only spirits dwell.

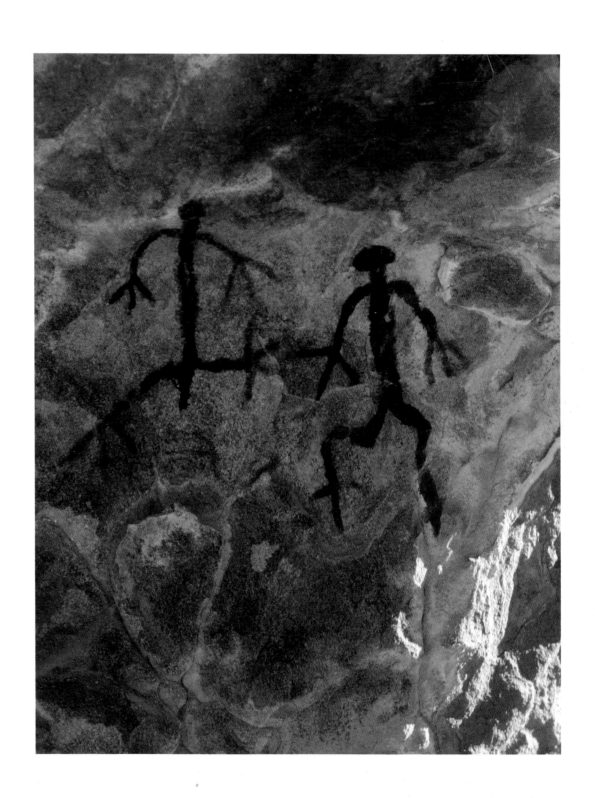

THE FORGOTTEN ARTIST

Even the most skeptical critic of pictographs and petroglyphs would admit that they are art, though of a different dimension. How does this primitive art fit into today's Native American society?

Although they do not practice rock art per se, American Indian artists today use some of the old motifs found in pictographs and petroglyphs. They weave these curvilinear and rectilinear symbols into baskets or paint them on pottery. Navajo sand paintings apparently evolved from painted murals dating to A.D. 1400–1600. Hopi kachina masks may have originated in petroglyphs and pictographs. And the ancient symbols have recently found their way back onto the modern canvases of Hopi and Navajo artists.

Non-Indian artists too have incorporated these prehistoric symbols in their work. In the 1940s, when American artists were searching for new art expression, they reworked elements from primitive art. Adolph Gottlieb's *Pictograph* and *Pictograph-Symbol*, both done in 1942, are examples. Also Joan Miro's *Woman Dreaming of Escape*, Jackson Pollock's *Guardian of the Secret*, and Theodoros Stamos's *Sounds in the Rock* also show this trend.

By the 1970s and 1980s, artists sought the natural domain of the primitive world. Robert Smithson created a work called *Spiral Jelly* in 1980. Located at the Great Salt Lake in Utah, its medium was black rock, salt crystals, soil and red water; it coiled 1,500 feet, and had it been done centuries ago it would have been classified as a geoglyph, intaglio, or ground figure. Richard Long's 1982 *River Avon Mud Circle* would be considered by rock art scholars to be symbolic concentric circles.

Primitive rock art, however, has not yet found its rightful place in the history of art in North America. Most art books contain a great deal of material on pottery, basketry, masks, and textiles, but the large murals in Canyonlands National Park in Utah, the polychrome pictographs of the Chumash Indians in southern California, and the art panels in Anza-Borrego have not yet received proper recognition.

The primitive artist may be forgotten by some, but his symbols and his spirit continue. The secrets of ritual, celebration, celestial events, and mystical journeys are held within the sacred rock caves of Anza-Borrego. The fascination and wonder they arouse will never fade. No doubt future archaeologists will pursue their investigations and unravel more secrets. But the whole story will be known only to the forgotten artist.

Bibliography

Almstedt, Ruth F. 1977. *Diegueño Curing Practices*. San Diego Museum Papers No. 10. San Diego: San Diego Museum of Man.

Applegate, Richard B. 1978. *Atishwin: The Dream Helper in South-Central California*. Ramona, Calif.: Ballena Press.

————. 1979. The Black, the Red, and the White: Duality and Unity in the Luiseño Cosmos. *Journal of California and Great Basin Anthropology*, vol. 1, no. 1, pp. 71–88.

Aschmann, Homer. 1967. *The Central Desert of Baja California: Demography and Ecology*. Riverside, Calif.: Manessier Publishing Company.

Barrett, S. A. 1952. *Material Aspects of Pomo Culture*. Milwaukee Public Museum Bulletin, no. 20.

Barrows, David P. 1900. *Ethno-Botany of the Coahuilla Indians*. Chicago: University of Chicago Press.

Bean, Lowell J. 1972. *Mukat's People. The Cahuilla Indians of Southern California*. Berkeley: University of California Press.

Bean, Lowell J., and Saubel, Katherine S. 1972. *Temalpakh*. Banning, Calif.: Malki Museum Press.

Begole, Robert. 1981. Investigations in the Anza-Borrego Desert State Park 1978–1980. *Pacific Coast Archaeology Society Quarterly*, vol. 17, no. 4, pp. 1–36.

Boas, Franz. 1955. *Primitive Art*. New York: Dover Publications.

Boscana, Father Geronimo. (1846)1933. *Chinigchinish*. A Revised and Annotated Version of Alfred Robinson's Translation of Father Geronimo Boscana's Historical Account of the Belief, Usages, Customs, and Extravagancies of the Indians of the Mission of San Juan Capistrano Called the Acagchemen Tribe. P. T. Hanna, ed. Santa Ana, Calif.: Fine Arts Press.

Carpenter, Edmund. 1978. Silent Music and Invisible Art. *Natural History*, vol. 87, no. 5.

Carter, George, 1957. *Pleistocene Man at San Diego*. Baltimore: Johns Hopkins Press.

Claiborne, Robert. 1973. *The First Americans*. New York: Time-Life Books.

Cline, Lora L. 1984. *Just Before Sunset*. Jacumba, Calif.: J. and L. Enterprises.

Crosby, Harry. 1984. *The Cave Paintings of Baja California*. San Diego: Copley Books.

Cuero, Delfina. 1970. *The Autobiography of Delfina Cuero: A Diegueño Indian*, as told to Florence C. Shipek. Rosalia Pinto, Interpreter. Banning, Calif.: Malki Museum Press.

Du Bois, Constance G. 1908. Ceremonies and Traditions of the Diegueño Indians. *Journal of American Folklore*, vol. 21, pp. 228–236.

————. 1908. *The Religion of the Luiseño Indians of Southern California*. University of California Publications in American Archaeology and Ethnology 8. Berkeley: University of California Press.

Eliade, Mircea. 1972. *Shamanism. Archaic Techniques of Ecstacy*. Bollingen Series 76. Princeton: Princeton University Press.

Frazer, Sir James George. 1955. *Spirits of the Corn and the Wild*. Third Edition of the Golden Bough: A Study in Magic and Religion. Part 5. New York: Avenel Books.

Furst, Peter T. 1974. The Roots and Continuities of Shamanism. In *Stones, Bones and Skin: Ritual and Shamanic Art*. Artscanada, vol. 30, no 5/6, pp. 33–60.

Giedion, Sigfried. 1962. *The Eternal Present: The Beginnings of Art*. Bollingen Series 35. New York: Pantheon Books.

Gifford, Edward W. 1931. *The Kamia of the Imperial Valley*. Washington, D.C.: Bureau of American Ethnology, Bulletin 97.

Grant, Campbell. 1965. *Rock Paintings of the Chumash*. Berkeley: University of California Press.

————. 1983. *Rock Art of the North American Indians*. Cambridge: Cambridge University Press.

Grant, Campbell; Baird, James W.; and Pringle, J. Kenneth. 1968. *Rock Drawings of the Coso Range*. China Lake, Calif.: Maturango Museum.

Harrington, John P. 1981. *The Eye of the Flute*. Chumash Traditional History and Ritual as Told by Fernando Librardo Kitsepawit to John P. Harrington. Banning, Calif.: Malki Museum Press.

Hedges, Kenneth. 1970. *An Analysis of Diegueño Pictographs*. Unpublished Master's Thesis. San Diego: San Diego State University.

————. 1973. Rock Art of Southern California. *Pacific Coast Archaeological Society Quarterly*, vol. 9, no. 4, pp. 1–28.

————. 1975. Notes on the Kumeyaay: A Problem of Identification. *The Journal of California Anthropology*, vol. 2, no. 10, pp. 71–83.

————. 1986. Personal Communications.

Heizer, Robert F. 1953. *Sacred Rain Rocks of Northern California*. University of California Archaeological Survey Reports, no. 20, pp. 33–38.

Heizer, Robert F., and Baumhoff, Martin A. 1962. *Prehistoric Rock Art of Nevada and Eastern California*. Berkeley: University of California Press.

Hooper, Lucille. 1920. *The Cahuilla Indians*. University of California Publications in Archaeology and Ethnology 16. Berkeley: University of California Press.

Hudson, Travis, and Underhay, Ernest. 1978. *Crystals in the Sky: An Intellectual Odyssey Involving Chumash Astronomy, Cosmology and Rock Art*. Ballena Press Anthropological Papers, no. 10.

Hudson, Travis; Lee, Georgia; and Hedges, Ken. 1979. Solstice Observers and Observatories in native California. *Journal of California and Great Basin Anthropology*, vol. 1, no. 1, pp. 38–63.

James, Harry. (1960)1969. *The Cahuilla Indians*. Reprint. Banning, Calif.: Malki Museum Press.

Kroeber, Alfred L. 1906. Two Myths of the Mission Indians of California. *Journal of American Folklore*, vol. 19, no. 75, pp. 309–321.

———. 1925. *Handbook of the Indians of California*. Washington, D.C.: Bureau of American Ethnology, Bulletin 78.

Leroi-Gourhan, André. 1968. The Evolution of Paleolithic Art. *Scientific American*, pp. 58–70. February.

Loeb, Edwin M. 1926. *Pomo Folkways*. University of California Publications in American Archaeology and Ethnology 19. Berkeley: University of California Press.

Lommel, Andreas. 1967. *Shamanism, The Beginnings of Art*. New York: McGraw-Hill.
Luomala, Katherine. 1978. "Tipai-Ipai." In *Handbook of the North American Indians*, Robert F. Heizer, ed., vol. 8, California. Washington, D.C.: Smithsonian Institution.

Mallery, Garrick. 1893. Picture Writing of the American Indians. Washington, D.C.: *Tenth Annual Report of the Bureau of Ethnology*, pp. 1–822.

Marshack, Alexander. 1972. *The Roots of Civilization: The Cognitive Beginnings of Man's First Art, Symbol and Notation*. New York: McGraw-Hill.

McGowan, Charlotte. 1982. *Ceremonial Fertility Sites in Southern California*. San Diego Museum Papers no. 14. San Diego: San Diego Museum of Man.

Meighan, Clement W. 1958. *Archaeological Resources of the Borrego Desert State Park*. Sacramento: Department of Parks and Recreation.

Minor, Rick. 1973. Known Origins of Rock Paintings of Southern California. *Pacific Coast Archaeological Society Quarterly*, vol. 9, no. 4, pp. 29-36.

———. 1975. *The Pit-and-Groove Petroglyph Style in Southern California*. Ethnic Technology Notes, no. 15. San Diego: Museum of Man.

Minshall, Herbert. 1976. *The Broken Stones*. San Diego: Copley Books.

Modesto, Ruby, and Mount, Guy. 1980. *Not For Innocent Ears*. Spiritual Tradition of a Desert Cahuilla Medicine Woman. Arcata, Calif.: Sweetlight Books.

Monson, Gale, and Sumner, Lowell. 1981. *The Desert Bighorn*. Its Life History, Ecology, and Management. Tucson: University of Arizona Press.

Mooney, James. 1965. *The Ghost Dance Religion*. Chicago: University of Chicago Press.

Moratto, Michael J. 1984. *California Archaeology*. New York: Academic Press.

Park, Willard Z. 1938. *Shamanism in Western North America*. Chicago: Northwestern University.

Patencio, Francisco. 1943. *Stories and Legends of the Palm Springs Indians*. Times-Mirror Press, Los Angeles.

Payen, Louis A. 1959. *Petroglyphs of Sacramento and Adjoining Counties, California*. University of California Archaeological Survey Reports, no. 48, pp. 66–83.

Rogers, Spencer L. 1976. Healing Practices of the Diegueño Indians. In *The People Cabrillo Met*. San Diego: Cabrillo Historical Association.

————. 1976. *The Shaman's Healing Way*. Ramona, Calif.: Acoma Books.

————. 1982. *The Shaman*. His Symbols and His Healing Power. Springfield, Ill.: Charles C. Thomas.

Sampson, Michael. 1984. *Test Excavations at Ca-SDi-813, Mine Canyon, Anza-Borrego Desert State Park*. Sacramento: Department of Parks and Recreation.

Schaafsma, Polly. 1980. *Indian Rock Art of the Southwest*. Santa Fe: School of American Research and, Albuquerque: University of New Mexico Press.

Shackley, Michael S. 1981. *Late Prehistoric Exchange Network Analysis in Carrizo Gorge and the Far Southwest*. Unpublished Master's Thesis. San Diego: San Diego State University.

Sorrel, Walter. 1973. *The Other Face: The Mask in the Arts*. New York: Bobbs-Merrill Company.

Sparkman, Philip S. 1908. *The Culture of the Luiseño Indians*. University of California Publications in American Archaeology and Ethnology 8. Berkeley: University of California Press.

Spier, Leslie. 1923. *Southern Diegueño Customs*. University of California Publications in American Archaeology and Ethnology 20. Berkeley: University of California Press.

Steward, Julian. 1929. *Petroglyphs of California and Adjoining States*. University of California Publications in Archaeology and Ethnology 24. Berkeley: University of California Press.

Strong, William D. 1929. *Aboriginal Society in Southern California*. University of California Publications in American Archaeology and Ethnology 26. Berkeley: University of California Press.

Taylor, R.E., and Payen, Louis A., et al. 1985. Major Revisions in the Pleistocene Assignments for North American Human Skeletons by C-14 Accelerator Mass Spectrometry: None Older Than 11,000 C-14 years B.P. *American Antiquity*, vol. 50, no. 1, pp. 136–139.

Van Camp, Gena R. 1979. *Kumeyaay Pottery. Paddle-and-Anvil Techniques of Southern California*. Ramona, Calif.: Ballena Press.

Varnedoe, Kirk. 1985. "Abstract Expressionism." In *Primitivism in 20th Century Art*, William Rubin, ed., vol. 2. New York: The Museum of Modern Art.

Vastokas, Joan, and Vastokas, Romas K. 1973. *Sacred Art of the Algonkians. A Study of the Peterborough Petroglyphs*. Peterborough, Ontario: Mansard Press.

Von Werlhof, Jay C. 1965. *Rock Art of the Owens Valley, California*. University of California Archeological Survey Reports, no. 65. Berkeley: University of California Press.

Wallace, William, and Taylor, Edith. 1958. An Archaeological Reconnaissance in Bow Willow Canyon, Anza-Borrego Desert State Park. *The Masterkey*, vol. 32, no. 5, pp. 155–166.

————. 1960. The Indian Hill Rockshelter Preliminary Excavations. *The Masterkey*, vol. 34, no. 2, pp. 66–82.

Waterman, Thomas T. 1909. Analysis of the Mission Indian Creation Story. *American Anthropologist*, vol. 11, pp. 41–55.

————. 1910. *The Religious Practices of the Diegueño Indians*. University of California Publications in American Archaeology and Ethnology 8. Berkeley: University of California Press.

Wilke, Philip J.; and Lawton, Harry W.; King, T. F.; Hammond, S. 1975. *The Cahuilla Indians of the Colorado Desert: Ethnohistory and Prehistory*. Ramona, Calif.: Ballena Press.

Wilke, Philip J.; and McDonald, Meg; Payen, L. A. 1986. *Excavations at Indian Hill Rockshelter Anza-Borrego Desert State Park, California 1984–1985*. Sacramento: California Department of Parks and Recreation.

Williamson, Ray A. 1981. "North America: A Multiplicity of Astronomies." In *Archaeoastronomy in the Americas*, Ray A. Williamson, ed. Los Altos, Calif.: Ballena Press.

112

Index

Numerals in italics indicate an illustration of the subject mentioned.

ABOUT THE AUTHOR

Manfred Knaak came to the United States in 1963 from Germany. His parents had settled in Immenstaad/Bodensee, after fleeing Danzig at the end of World War II. He began to travel in Baja California and the South-west, studying native cultures and realizing his childhood dream of learning about American Indians and the West.

He taught himself English, and earned a Bachelor's and Master's Degree in Anthropology from the San Diego State University. In 1972 Manfred was hired by Anza-Borrego Desert State Park to document Native American sites. In 1975 he became a State Park Ranger and has spent most of his career at Anza-Borrego studying the park's Native American cultures. He lives in Borrego Springs with his wife Betsy.

PHOTO CREDITS

Bill Evarts
(10, 11, 12, 15, 22, 26, 94, 95)

Paul R. Johnson
(16, 24 top, 84)

Mark C. Jorgensen
(5)

Manfred Knaak
(ii, vi, viii, xiii, 7, 17, 18, 24 bottom, 27, 29, 32, 37, 40, 41, 42, 46, 47, 48, 49, 50, 52, 54, 58, 59, 62, 63, 64, 65, 75, 76, 79, 81, 82, 87, 89, 90, 91, 100, 101, 102, 103, 104)

Larry Ulrich
(4, 25, 68)

The Anza-Borrego Desert Natural History Association is a non-profit corporation dedicated to educational and interpretive activities and to the promotion of historical and scientific endeavors pertinent to the Anza-Borrego Desert State Park. It undertakes these objectives in close cooperation with the California Department of Parks and Recreation.

Published by Anza-Borrego Desert Natural History Association P.O. Box 311, Borrego Springs, California 92004
Book Design: Donaldson/Mahan
Maps and Illustrations: Michael Donaldson
Editorial: Rose Houk, Harry Daniel and Mark Jorgensen
Printing: Lorraine Press, Salt Lake City
Production: Betsy Knaak and Bob Petersen

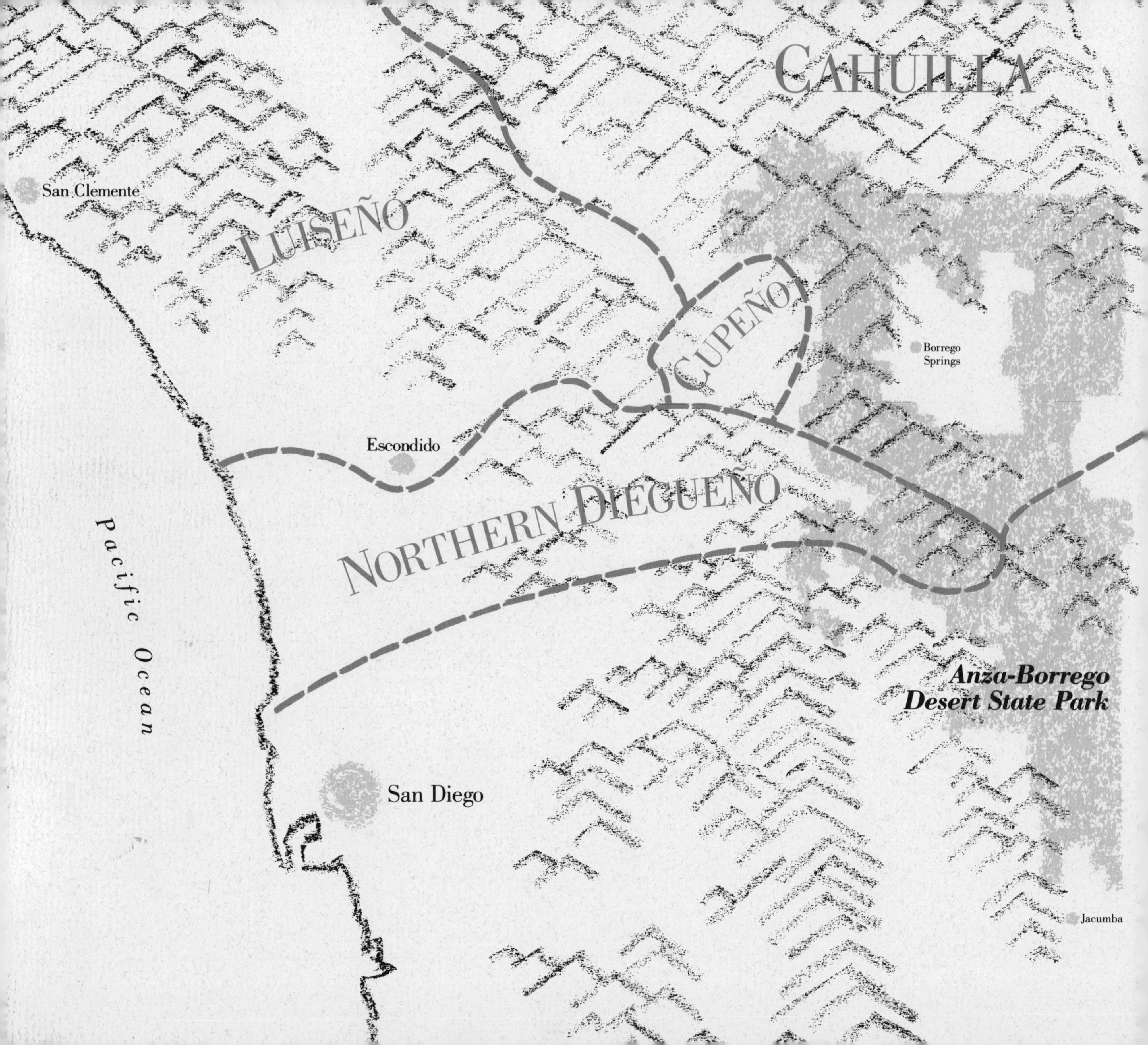

CAHUILLA

San Clemente

LUISEÑO

CUPEÑO

Borrego
Springs

Escondido

NORTHERN DIEGUEÑO

Pacific Ocean

**Anza-Borrego
Desert State Park**

San Diego

Jacumba